The Love of Baseball

The Love of Baseball

Essays by Lifelong Fans

Edited by CHRIS ARVIDSON
and DIANA NELSON JONES

McFarland & Company, Inc., Publishers
Jefferson, North Carolina

Library of Congress Cataloguing-in-Publication Data

Names: Arvidson, Christopher, editor.
Title: The love of baseball : essays by lifelong fans / Edited by Chris
    Arvidson and Diana Nelson Jones.
Description: Jefferson, North Carolina : McFarland & Company, Inc.,
    Publishers, 2017 | Includes index.
Identifiers: LCCN 2017030129 | ISBN 9781476669830 (softcover : acid
    free paper) ∞
Subjects: LCSH: Baseball fans. | Baseball—History.
Classification: LCC GV867.3 .L68 2017 | DDC 796.357—dc23
LC record available at https://lccn.loc.gov/2017030129

British Library cataloguing data are available

ISBN 978-1-4766-6983-0 (print)
ISBN 978-1-4766-3032-8 (ebook)

Front cover: Safeco Field in Seattle, Washington, photograph
by Mark B. Bauschke (Shutterstock)

Printed in the United States of America

McFarland & Company, Inc., Publishers
  Box 611, Jefferson, North Carolina 28640
  www.mcfarlandpub.com

Table of Contents

"How can you not be romantic about baseball?"
—Billy Beane

Preface

CHRIS ARVIDSON *and* DIANA NELSON JONES

We met over a piece of baseball writing. Diana, a longtime reporter and columnist for the *Pittsburgh Post-Gazette*, wrote about Chris' favorite Pirate that season, catcher Jason Kendall. He was not a big guy for a catcher, but he was scrappy and gritty and fun as hell to watch.

Because she was new to the city, Chris didn't have any Pirates buddies to commiserate with, so having that column appear in the newspaper felt like a real gift. Plus it didn't hurt that Diana was clearly "baseball people" and her love for the game and her team shone through the writing. Chris searched out Diana's email at the paper and sent her a fan letter about the column. The rest is baseball freak history.

Over the years, the two of us have gone to Pirates games together at Three Rivers Stadium and PNC Park. We haven't lived in the same town in more than a decade, but we've stayed in touch, mostly electronically. Our lives have gone in a hundred different directions, but we're still yakking on Facebook about our teams. As writers and super-fans, it was only natural for us to get together on a book about baseball—about why people, like us, love it so much.

In these pages we've put together the writing of friends, colleagues, friends-of-friends, classmates, and all manner of people we've run across over the years who share our baseball love. The book, in a way, is an extension of that conversation we baseball fans have all had. You know the one. A new acquaintance or maybe even someone you've known for a long time, says something about a game, a team, a player, and you realize you've found a kindred spirit. Another baseball freak. A wearer of MLB gear. A flyer of team flags. Someone who loves baseball like you do.

We've organized the writings like a baseball season. We begin with stories about the hope and eternal optimism of Spring Training, follow it with the guts and the grind of the baseball season proper, and then wind up with writing about the anticipation, heartbreak, and the glory of post-season play.

We all have stories about how we've come to love baseball, and why we continue to love it so. In these pages we're sharing some of these tales and we hope you enjoy them as much as we have in bringing them together.

PART I

Spring Training

The phrase *hope springs eternal* works wonderfully for the beginning of the baseball season. Spring training is the hope of a new year—everything is possible for our teams. Injuries have healed. The bad taste of last year's end-of-season slump is long gone. No more sour grapes. All is new spring wine.

Spring is also reminiscent of the beginnings of our love of baseball in general, and calls to mind the first days warm enough for us kids to step outside and clear off the snow, toss a ball between friends and dig the bats out of the garage. It's setting up our teams for the coming summer and maybe watching the local college players take their turns at bat. It's remembering being a kid and standing at home plate in our imaginations, taking that mighty game-winning swing...

Somewhere the Sun Is Shining

Diana Nelson Jones

Blue blue skies, wafty clouds like a jet's trail. And those palm trees. They line the outfield wall.

How can a high fly ball that hangs above a band of swaying palms not look more like a baseball than a high fly framed by red seats on a brisk, cloudy night in the Rust Belt? Are we fans really romantics, or does good sense draw the line here? How can this green grass and breezy sweetness of an 80-degree afternoon in March be the remarkable perception point?

Isn't everyone a romantic under these conditions?

* * *

Back when there were 44 days before pitchers and catchers would report to spring training, the year had just begun and the skies were brutish, maybe blowing snow in the fan's northern city. The fan, who could be any fan in any northern city, begins considering booking a flight to Florida. She checks the Spring Training schedule to book several days of home games into a 5-day trip.

The night before one such trip, four inches of snow-rain-sleet-slush have begun encrusting the earth and another eight are predicted through the night. An hour before midnight, like a caged-dog with rabies, the fan finishes packing and flees her warm home to trawl through a misty sleet, the carry-on full of shorts, T-shirts, sun block and paperbacks beside her on the seat.

It seems crazy for her to be doing this, but it would be crazier to miss that 8 a.m. flight to Florida.

The little car is a skiff cutting through the crackly, slidy detritus of a God-forsaken ocean. It seems the world is flat and that, not being able to see the drop-off, she is surely on the edge of it.

Holding her breath and going 30 mph all the way, she exhales when the ghostly parking lot lights of the airport blur the air up ahead.

The airport at this hour has the hum of a giant refrigerator, a thick layer of white noise over silence, with a janitor pushing a sweeper and zombie people in warm-up suits sitting at the Roy Rogers. Looking to find a place to sack out, the fan spots a flight attendant pulling a wheeled suitcase across the concourse.

"Have you tried the mezzanine?" the flight attendant asks. "A bunch of people up there look pretty comfortable."

Up the escalator and around a corner, bodies lie everywhere: a man on his coat with his knees sticking up, his hands over the wide part of his tie; another man on an overturned couch. A woman on her back on an overturned couch, her ankles crossed and her arms clutching her purse to her chest. Someone is breathing as though he had a referee's whistle clamped in his teeth. Several people take the form of question marks under heavy coats.

The fan sets off person-alert sensors as she looks for an empty space. Eyes open then close again. She drags a couch and props it against a stretch of wall, scrunching the carry-on into a pillow and begins breathing for the first time in what seems like hours. Then the wake up call: the smell of coffee, the sound of Muzak, things being flipped on and humming. The next leg of the journey to baseball.

*   *   *

The motel is not on the beach this time, but the beach can wait. Late morning light floods the room, where the fan becomes a human hurricane, trading jeans and sweater for shorts and a T-shirt. Boots off, flip-flops on. Into the radiant sunshine, into the rental car, up Manatee Avenue, hanging a left onto Ninth Street West, she catches the sob before it floods her body, blinks back tears.

Tears!

She power-walks toward McKechnie Field, then begins to jog, because the battery recharger is just inside the gate, where the pretty old lady tears the ticket and smiles, her Pirates' Ping-Pong earrings bouncing. And the fan leaps inside—safe!

A cheer goes up.

The Pirates are coming to bat, but the fan pretends the cheer is for her, having rounded the bases of winter and finally safe at home. She takes her seat, within spitting distance of the first base coach who whips his hands together as the line of palm trees move like feather dusters over the sky.

An old guy nearby is keeping score on a homemade tablet. He leaves room for at least five names between each starter.

"I admire you for keeping score in Spring Training," the fan tells him.

"It is sort of a clown convention, isn't it?" he says, chuckling. "But somma these guys ya never heard of? They'll be famous one day."

"Some'll be 28 and wondering whether Dad's tire business isn't such a bad deal after all," the fan says, fielding a reproachful look.

"Ah c'mon, don't say that," the scorekeeper says. "Not here." As he notes a foul tip with a little line by the batter's name, he says, "Talk to ya between innings."

*   *   *

A lot of people stitch some magic when they sew a baseball tale, and it's tempting when you're so unexpectedly warm and happy for five days in March, when you believe in the transcendence of the game, feel it so much you get teary.

But what's magic about Spring Training is that it's so real. Yes, neon green grass, but also an intimacy that lets you see faces you felt so familiar with. Once you see them in a Grapefruit League park, you realize you haven't really seen them before.

Someone yells a player's name and he looks up, really looks, and even smiles. Young players stroll by, looking beefy and brusque, stealing glances at the crowd of 10,000, and you can almost hear them thinking, "wow." They look very tender very briefly.

A coach walks along the first base line toward the bullpen and stops to chat with an old couple who are regulars, a couple who moved to Florida from the northern city years ago.

Between innings, the old scorekeeper asks the fan if she's cold because the air that seemed so warm has a little bite to it now that there's a stiff breeze.

"No," she says. "I've been cold and this isn't it."

"Where do you live?"

She tells him and asks, "Where are you from?"

"All over," he says, "but where I was cold was New York."

"Yankees or Mets?" she asks and he says, "Pirates now."

*   *   *

In Spring Training, it really doesn't matter who wins. Wins and losses don't indicate how the season will play out. Spring Training is rehearsal, and the fan gets to be backstage. One novice bobbles a grounder that another novice grabs to get the runner out. A new pitcher comes in every two innings. An exciting game is a messy game. The real payoff is that the games are played close to players, with a bright sun and blue sky overhead.

Before the fan's flight back north, at the last game of the week, a woman to whom she has been talking between innings turns to her and says, "This game could go on all day and I'd be happy to sit here watching it." The fan concurs. It is 82 degrees and those white legs that looked as if dusted in flour five days ago look season ready.

Back home, a friend asks the fan "Who looks good?" and the fan says, "Down there, they all do."

* * *

Baseball seasons are a series of specific measurements and analyses. Baseball players, like classical poets, work to a system of rhythms and lines. But a few transcend those forms—they are poetry in motion. Many inspire both the young and the old fans, and clubs have been known to grow up around them.

Fan clubs for baseball players abounded in the late 1960s. Some claimed to be official, which I assumed meant that they had some sanction from the team and the player, but most were free-form, made up by kids to honor their heroes.

You could find them in ads in the backs of sports magazines. One ad was mine, for an unofficial Roberto Clemente Fan Club. Its home base was a little post office box in Shinnston, WV. The post office was a '30s era, squat brick building on a side street of the town where that universal post-office smell locked into my sensory archive and it would forever trigger happy flashbacks of trips to get the mail with my dad.

He drove me there every day or two the summer of 1969 to collect the growing numbers of envelopes. He let me roll the dial to unlock our code to get into the decorative brass box. You could see the treasure through the little window in the middle.

The first 20 fan club members were obliging classmates, some of whom joined out of friendship if not fanship, but then the mail began arriving. It came from Dunkirk, NY; Janesville, WI; Santa Ana, CA; Cincinnati; Ft. Gibson, OK; Orlando; Toms River, NJ; Cranston, RI; New York City; Glenham, SD; Hannibal, OH; Dorval in Quebec; Waycross, GA; Brenham, TX; Portland, OR; Urbana, IL; Pontiac, MI; Madisonville, TN; St. Louis; Alexandria, VA; Le Mars, IA; Blaine, WA; Lakin, KS; Taunton, MA; Charlotte, NC; several Rochesters; Wilmington, DE; and dozens and dozens from Pittsburgh and western Pennsylvania. There were more than 200 members by 1970.

My parents went on and on about the reach of my little club. My dad opened the book of maps to find some of the places. He propped his glasses up and leaned his head back with his finger on the state of Michigan: "Where the hell is Swartz Creek?" he mused, not finding it before starting to look for Ironwood.

He studied my list, saying some of the names of kids whose ethnicity we knew nothing of in our little town in the coalfields. We had some favorite names—Winky Easley, Sherri Stringfellow and Angel San Martin among them. An inveterate letter writer, I struck up pen pal relationships with a few of them.

"Vacaville, California!" Daddy exclaimed. "I knew a guy from there in the Army at Fort Sill." When a letter arrived from Santurce, PR, I put a star by that name on my member list. Santurce was where Roberto had played before he hit the majors.

As my fan member base grew, I felt as if I had parted a curtain on a whole new world outside my little town. With the club, I had unlocked the power of putting an ad in a sports magazine, enticing all these kids to invest hard-earned dues of six-cent stamps for future newsletters.

Of course, Roberto was the enticement. Their responses were vindication that I had chosen THE player as my baseball hero. I felt the pressure of making their membership meaningful. At age 11, I had my first writing job with deadlines.

The 6-cent stamps represented the number of newsletters a person wanted to sign up for. The newsletters, as I remember, were monthly. They included copied professional articles about Roberto and the Pirates as well as my own commentary about the Pirates, Roberto and their season. The newsletters included announcements, lists of members' birthdates, their stories about baseball—especially about Roberto—and articles and drawings from their own hometown papers.

I figured at the time that most of the respondents were children like me, but now as I peruse the yellowed list of members, I wonder.

*   *   *

Roberto Clemente caught my attention the way he caught the attention of the legion of fans who proclaimed him their favorite player. I didn't just watch him on the little TV at home. I studied him. And when the day came for me to see him in person for the first time, I jittered in the backseat the whole three-hour ride up Route 19 to Forbes Field. It was May 12, 1968, and we got there early.

Of course we sat in right field and I held my breath when I spotted him. On the field below, he sprinted, he paced, he played catch with teammates, he rolled his head in a circle from one shoulder to the other. I glanced briefly at the Longines clock in left field and at the tall building beyond—the Cathedral of Learning—but I was otherwise mesmerized by the sight of Roberto, and that was before the game even started.

During the game, I saw in person what the TV had only hinted at. My mother had said he was handsome. I thought that was a very limited assessment.

Roberto was a master of physical poetry, a man of great beauty and enigma. His compact body seemed to be locked around a taut spring. Energy sparked from him when he walked, even when he stood in the on deck circle. When he threw a ball from the outfield, he channeled Rudolph Nureyev.

There may have been greater players before him and since, but few if any whose presentation was sheer, sensory magic.

My first live game didn't even last as long as the drive to Pittsburgh. The Pirates beat the Phillies 2–1 in one hour and 55 minutes. But the milestone has lasted my lifetime.

*   *   *

One member of my fan club, David Sheagley from Hoopstown, IL, shared a story that I printed in the newsletter: "My father and my two brothers and I went to Chicago the 12th and 13th to see the Bucs play the Cubs. After the Saturday game, we went to the Holiday Inn and got a room for the night. My older brother and I went over to the Executive House where Roberto and the Pirates were staying. Eric decided to call up to his room from the lobby. Roberto picked up the phone. The next morning we had breakfast with him, and he said to be sure to get his attention when he goes out on the field today. It was raining and they didn't know whether they'd have the game, but Roberto was the first one out on the field. He asked us to come out for a photograph."

David sent me the photo of himself and his brother with Roberto. In the many years since, I have learned of Roberto's largesse with fans, and have my own modest experience.

My dad procured tickets for the game on Aug. 18, 1968. The night before, Mother granted me an old bed sheet, and I got out my permanent markers and a Spanish dictionary to look up the words for "happy birthday" and began making a sign to hold up the next day.

From our perch in right field, I unfurled the sign, which read "Feliz cumpleanos, Roberto!!!" He was stretching his neck and I was bouncing the sign when his teammate, Jose Pagan, nudged his arm and pointed up at me.

Roberto looked up. He smiled and took off his cap and waved it at me, and I think my father had to hold the top of my shorts to keep me from flying off the upper tier.

Our family would return to Forbes Field several more times, and when the field was torn down, we attended a few games at Three Rivers Stadium. After Roberto's death on New Year's Eve, 1972, in a plane that should never have taken flight, I did not see another baseball game until I was well into adulthood.

It wasn't a reaction to losing him. I was just grown up and moving on.

The city that held such special charm and magic for me then is the city I live in today, where I work at the Pittsburgh *Post-Gazette*. In 1997, I talked my editor into letting me go to Puerto Rico to summon stories about Roberto from people he knew there. The story would run to commemorate the 35th year of his passing.

I knew no Spanish then, but I asked a friend who did to coach me on how to say certain things. One of the sentences I learned, in fact memorized, I delivered to Roberto's widow, Vera, when I met her at her home during my trip.

"Cuando era una niña, tenia un club por los aficionados de Roberto," I told her: When I was a girl, I had a fan club for Roberto. Her face suddenly went from well-ordered to meltdown. With a huge smile, and then, with a tilt of her head, she gave me a hug.

We visited the beach where she held vigil in the days following the crash of the plane into the ocean. She took us for empanadas at the roadside food stands that she and Roberto used to go to. She showed us the church where they were married.

I came back and began taking Spanish lessons in a city where Spanish is hard to find and where Roberto's presence now is an effort of the imagination. I realized the sky that always seemed to threaten rain to me as a kid was really just dirty back then.

I know that my choice of baseball hero was an exquisite one and that what I saw as a child showed real discernment. But it is safe to assume that somewhere, today, a kid is studying a player, mesmerized by a magic that she and many others can see, a magic that is without peer.

I now go to games under a mostly blue sky, and I watch players who are physical marvels, masters of technique and physique. But in none is there a hint of what I saw in Roberto.

I will never be that lucky again.

Opening Days

Glenn B. Marcus

On April 15, 1954, before I headed out to first grade that spring day, mom reminded me my father would pull me out of school early to take me to a game, and that the teacher would remind me when it was time to go outside and wait for the family car to pull up. When I mentioned this to my classmates, one of them said, "I wish I could go to Opening Day." Only when Dad and I pulled up in front of the new Memorial Stadium in Baltimore did I have any idea at all what "Opening Day" meant. In this case it was the first opening day—the home game of the new Baltimore Orioles franchise. The big crowd, banners and bands, speechifying and introductions, the hot dogs, popcorn, peanuts, and of course Cracker Jacks all made big impressions. The grass was so perfect, the scoreboard so big, and Dad showing me how he used the scorecard was confusing yet comforting—he knew everything, and someday, I might too. The home team was victorious on that monumental day, and briefly moved into first place. A quip emerged from that momentary glory—"and that was the last game they won the whole year." Not quite, but the team did lose 100 games, and there was no place to go but up. My love affair had begun, thanks to Dad.

He had a professional association with the team and worked many games; I only got to sit with him on special occasions. 1958 was extra special. The All-Star game came to Baltimore for the first time. Dad and I were sitting in temporary box seats on the right field line during batting practice, before he had to get up to the press box. Left-handed Pirates hitter Bob Skinner was in the cage and Dad said, "This guy might hit a liner here, get ready." And he did. Dad was a terrific athlete—he had been captain of the 1938 West Virginia University basketball team, where he had actually played against the legendary Red Auerbach—and he leaped and speared a line shot, but it plopped right out of the lap of the older woman sitting next to us. She was none too thrilled, until my dad presented the ball to her and her husband, who turned out to be a City Councilman and union organizer, an elegant and forgiving man in a three-piece suit. Dad consoled me. "I'll get you another one sometime," and he did, often with autographs. He got back from working in the press box by the seventh inning, just in time for the entire stadium to rise as one, cheering at top volume. I then noticed a lone figure was walking in from the right field bullpen, directly in front of us, with his warm-up jacket flung over the shoulder. Indeed, it was Orioles pitching star Billy O'Dell, who shut the National League down in order for the last three innings, preserving the victory. Willie Mays, Ted Williams, Mickey Mantle, Stan Musial, Baltimore born and bred Al Kaline, and other superstars were there that day, but our guy was the unforgettable man of the hour. Amazingly, equally exciting was a game late that September, when Dad was able to sit with me for one full game of a Yankees series. We were close enough that I imagined actually seeing the movements of the legendary Hoyt Wilhelm's knuckleball. I certainly sensed the frustration of the enemy hitters flailing at the flutterball, and from the middle innings on, the buzz in the crowd got ever louder as the zeros and K's mounted. Finally, a thunderous cheer erupted as his no-hitter was completed, and our hero was mobbed as he headed to the dugout. Turns out this remains the last time a pitcher threw a complete game no hitter against the Bronx bombers.

Nineteen fifty-nine brought another milestone. On a sweltering June evening, Cleveland's Rocky Colavito had hit two home runs, when in his third time up, the bat flew out of his hands and into the stands. He homered thereafter, and in his last plate appearance, entered the hallowed halls of those to hit four home runs in a game, to the delight even of the home crowd. The next day, reading about it, the phrase "lady killer" was one of the descriptors of the record-tying outfielder. I said to my father with alarm, "Was a woman killed by the bat into the stands?" He smiled and told me that the expression meant Colavito was a handsome man popular with the ladies, and that no one had been hurt. I was relieved, though still didn't quite get it.

Happily, I attended high school literally in the shadow of the stadium, back when there were several day games early in the season, to keep the crowds from suffering shivering nights. Many of us would get an excuse for the last period and head over. We would pool our money so everyone could afford lots of food and drink, and when a slugger stepped to the plate, we often moved to the appropriate spot in the bleachers hoping for a home-run ball. My friend John still has to hear me tell the story occasionally of the time I pointed out a row and seat one of us needed to get to for a certain batter, but before we got there, the hitter crushed one that landed exactly on that seat. I pretty much stopped "calling" things then, resting on that inexplicable laurel. Dad would give the boys from my neighborhood a ride home. He was a legendary driver and route planner—having directed traffic off Omaha

Beach and beyond during the war, and the boys loved him. That was the source of some of my popularity, but I didn't mind.

The Orioles had an extraordinary "almost" season in 1960, and "Oriole magic" hit its first peak with the 4–0 sweep of the LA Dodgers in the 1966 World-Series. Our four young fireballers were able to outduel the LA Hall of Famers Don Drysdale and Sandy Koufax, pitching his very last game. One sportswriter wrote that the Dodgers were now being given the "penultimate baseball insult—they could not hit the fastball." I looked up "penultimate," and then asked Dad what the ultimate insult would be. He answered, "to choke."

Most people know that the great American pastime lends itself well to literature, producing more books, including many by revered writers, than most any other subject in the American pantheon. To me, baseball writing was a wonderful education. To say nothing of the many baseball movies, some from those books, but many original screenplays and TV dramas. Pastoral dreams, renewal, civic pride, cultural divides, even science fiction—they are all there in spades.

Occasionally, Dad would let me come up to the press box where he was monitoring commercials on radio. This allowed me to meet some future Hall of Fame sports broadcasters like Ernie Harwell, later of the Tigers and the legendary Chuck Thompson, who also broadcast for the Baltimore Colts. Thompson famously called the last play of the 1958 NFL overtime championship game between the Colts and the Giants, which was often credited by many for elevating pro football to a much higher level of popularity than it previously enjoyed. That same fateful year, one of the O's broadcasters, the handsome and charming Bailey Goss, was killed in an auto accident, the first person I knew who died that way. It was said that the other driver was drinking. I imagined someone distracted by having a soda or coffee in his hand—only later did I realize the deadly nature of "drinking and driving." My reverence for announcers served me in good stead later, during my career making documentary films, where the narration is critical and my work in scripting and narration supervision was especially rewarding. Some of that film work involved sports figures talking about their war experiences. Like my Dad, Hoyt Wilhelm and Hall of Fame Braves pitcher Warren Spahn, had suffered through the Battle of the Bulge, which had the most casualties of any battle in all of U.S. history, and took place during the coldest European winter in 50 years. As Casey Stengel would say "You can look it up." Spahn told us: "I was from Buffalo, I thought I knew cold. But I didn't really know cold until the Battle of the Bulge." During his playing days, he was once asked if he felt pressure before a big game. "Not at all. Pressure is fighting the Nazis." Ted Williams told us about being John Glenn's wingman in Korea, and Yogi Berra recalled his boat coming right up to Omaha Beach on June 6, 1944. The baseball gods blessed me in so many ways.

I had stayed in my hometown for college, at Johns Hopkins, where the housing was also within easy striking distance of the stadium. While most of my buddies went away, my explanations for attending a local school ranged from "my parole agreement required me to stay in the city," to the less unbelievable "I could not leave the Orioles or the Baltimore Colts," for whom Dad also toiled (don't get me started on the Irsay family, who cravenly stole the Colts in the middle of the night for Indianapolis). My loyalty to the Colts had been very strong, and many may have seen the iconic breakthrough feature film of Oscar winner Barry Levinson, *Diner*, in which a fiancée had to pass a Colts trivia test before the marriage could go forward. While a good but not great athlete, I looked like a pro QB when tossing the ball around, as my father's work friend, the steely John Unitas, had shown me how to drop back and then throw properly. And, yes, Brooks Robinson once gave me a quick tutorial on fielding a ground ball. Those were also the days when ballplayers lived in the city, had businesses such as restaurants, car dealerships, or sports stores, and would come to your little league parade and attend the father-son dinner at your church or synagogue. Yes, they were local celebrities, but approachable and low key. In fact, the immensely likeable Brooks made an unforgettable public service commercial in which he said, "A man never stands so tall as when he stoops to help a boy."

There was then the heartbreak of the 1969 World Series to the "Amazin' Mets," redemption in 1970 against the seemingly unbeatable "Big Red Machine," a loss to the great and lamented Roberto Clemente and his Pirates in 1971, to the "We are Family" Pittsburghers again in 1979, led by Willie Stargell, and the gawky reliever Kent Tekulve, whose unathletic appearance was celebrated by the great Nora Ephron for looking like anything but a star. Nineteen eighty-three brought the last Orioles ascendancy, in a World Series victory over the Philadelphia Phillies led by Cy Young Award winner Steve Carlton, known for his mastery of martial arts and refusal to speak with the press. That series was also in effect the first triumph on the national stage for Orioles MVP and future iron man shortstop Cal Ripken, Jr., in the third year of his historic career. I had seen Cal throwing the ball around as a 12-year old, and he looked pretty good, but who knew? Years later, I attended the game in which he tied Lou Gehrig's record for most consecutive games played—a record never expected to be broken—but gave my ticket up for the record setting next game. I had witnessed many a famous baseball moment, so this one would go to someone who never had. I did get to see the very last game of Ripken's career, and share that with my fellow baseball lover Elwin, who had made his first wages as a batboy for the Wesleyan University nine.

While the 1983 series win was memorable, a regular season game topped that year for me. In the 10th inning at home in August, ace left-handed reliever Tippy Martinez was on the mound for the O's, but they had run out of catchers, and utility infielder Len Sakata was pressed into service behind the plate. Three consecutive Seattle Mariners reached first base, and each one took a large lead, assuming they could swipe second on the inexperienced Sakata. And, as I like to say, you never ever have to make anything up—the real world gives you enough amazing tales. So yes, each one of those greedy runners was picked off by Martinez, and yes, in the bottom of the inning, the insulted Sakata homered to win it, making Martinez the rare winning pitcher to claim a victory without retiring a batter. Of course as always, I called my father right afterward to discuss the game. I think many of the calls I placed to him in my adulthood were spurred by sports moments. When he passed away, my mother took great comfort in keeping up with the Orioles, "my boys," as she called them. For a special birthday one year, my brother Warren and I drove up from DC, picked her up at our childhood home where she still lived, and headed to a game at Camden Yards. In the middle of the fourth inning, the scoreboard flashed "Happy 80th Birthday Marion Marcus." She was thrilled, and we all held back tears. Mom had also loved the antics of the '70s and '80s taxi driver Wild Bill Hagy, who led his iconic O-R-I-O-L-E-S cheer with his scraggly gray beard and cowboy hat from the upper deck (which can still be seen on YouTube). And, we thought it would be OK to lure the O's Bird Mascot to come down that day and put her head in his beak as was his wont. She was greatly amused.

I have lived in Washington, D.C., for 45 years—from Nixon to Trump—and gained many new Oriole fan friends who knew the O's as their only team, D.C. having lost two franchises that century. When the Montreal Expos moved here to become the current Washington Nationals, I now had two teams to root for—one in each league. The Nationals played in the old RFK stadium while waiting for the promised new ballpark to be completed. In their last season there, I had met a girl with whom I was totally enamored. For our second date, she asked if I were a baseball fan. My heart soared as I responded with an emphatic "absolutely." She added that she had four tickets from her firm, and that no one else was interested in this late season game and did I have any baseball fan friends who might want to join us. "Absolutely." I recruited two close friends to come along, in part to show her I had friends, and that they were nice. Brian, a Mets fan, and Elliott an Indians fan, who both share with me the love of the game beyond their own teams, were told that this hapless Nats game mattered a lot to me, so "come on down." We three boys got there early, and when my date appeared, flashed that smile which has dazzled me from the very first moment, and proceeded to sit down and start filling out a scorecard, my friends looked at me with expressions that said clearly, "my friend, you are so hooked, and rightly so." There were more dates to come, and we have been happily married for years now. Our only regret is that neither of our baseball loving fathers—our scorecard teachers—lived to see our nuptials. Thankfully, my mother was able to walk down the aisle on our wedding day, understanding the baseball bond. It was hers, too. In the end, she knew that attending a game is much about just being outside with friends and family in a colorful setting, maybe with a brew or two. And of course by now I imagine Mom and Dad watching a game together in the great beyond, though possibly with a martini rather than a beer.

My wife, a lifelong Phillies fan, has now adopted the Nats, and we share season tickets with a group of friends. However, if the Orioles were going nowhere, and played a game that meant a lot more to the Nats, I would still cheer for my O's. After all, I still have to root with Dad. And Mom.

Throw Like a Girl

Rebecca Bratcher Laxton

It's just a few weeks before baseball season when spring finally arrives in the Pocono Mountains of Pennsylvania, emancipating us from our stiff coats, snow pants and boots. My friends and I sit outside in the warm sunshine waiting for the school day to begin, listening to music, and surveying our kingdom. As sixth graders, we rule the school.

My cassette tape of Billy Joel's "Glass Houses" plays on my tape recorder. I rewind and pause the cassette while Kathy writes down the lyrics in her notebook so we can sing along. Amy arrives late, so she races across the playground and bounds up the steps two at a time to where we sit.

"Hey!" She tries to yell over the song. We look up to see a slightly disheveled Amy towering over us. Her shirt flies about partially untucked and one of her tube socks slides down her leg. "Pause that," she yells, out of breath from her sprint across the playground.

I hit the pause button on the tape recorder. "Jeez Amy, what's up? Why are you running and screaming?"

"I'm not screaming. Your music is too loud." She pauses, still catching her breath. "But, I wanted to remind you guys about baseball tryouts. We only have a few days left to get you guys ready. My dad says he can practice with us on Saturday." Her eyes are wide and she tries to smile, but it comes out looking like a strange Cheshire catlike grimace. She shifts her weight from one leg to the other and looks back and forth at the three of us sitting next to each other on the stairs.

I sit with my elbow on my knee, resting my head on my palm which was covering my mouth, Kathy's hand shields her eyes like a cap, blocking the sun as she stares up at Amy, and Wendy sits with her elbows on her knees and her hands propping up both sides of her head. Her hands rest slightly over her ears. I laugh thinking that we resemble the "hear no evil, see no evil, say no evil" monkeys.

17

"Sit down, Amy, before you give yourself a heart attack." I scoot over and slap my hand next to me on the metal stair, hoping she'll relax and sit down.

"This is serious. Stop laughing," Her voice gets louder. "You guys said you'd try out. They have to let you play if you're good enough." She takes a breath and continues. "The Little League didn't let my sister play when she was twelve, because she's a girl; can you believe it?" Amy, the youngest in a family of athletes, is very competitive. When we were taking the Presidential Fitness Test in gym class, Amy and Mike decided to have a chin up contest. Mike did eight chin-ups and we clapped and cheered. When he jumped down, Amy walked over to the chin up bar, pulled herself up and did nine. Only the girls were cheering though.

"Sit down, Amy," says Wendy. "I'm going to try out, I'm pretty sure, but I have to make sure I can get a ride." Amy collapses onto the stair in front of us.

"I'm trying out for sure." I grin. "My brother said I could use his old glove and we've been practicing. My whole family has been practicing."

On the weekends my dad comes home, we walk to the baseball field that sits behind my house, and practice hitting, throwing and catching. Everyone joins in—my mom, dad, brother and sister. I think we all want to spend time with our dad. He and our mom separated over a year ago, but playing baseball together seems to remind him how much fun it is to be a family. I know he would be proud if I made the team. Maybe he would even come home for good so he could see the weekday games.

Amy exclaims, "That's good. I know you'll make it Becky." We all turn to look at Kathy.

"I don't think my parents will let me," she mumbles. Her hand still shields her eyes.

"Have you asked them? Maybe they'll surprise you and be okay with it," I say.

"I don't think so. They almost didn't let me run on the relay team, remember? And that was all girls. Mr. U talked them into it. They don't really think girls should play on the same team as the boys. My brother Bobby plays baseball, and I'm faster than Bobby. That would be weird."

"Maybe my dad can talk to them and explain that they passed a law a few years ago so that girls could play in the Little League," Amy says.

"Well, just because there is a law that lets girls play doesn't mean my dad will let me," Kathy says. She stares at her notebook as she speaks and whacks it with her pencil. The teacher's aide rings the bell and we obediently make our way down the stairs and across the blacktop playground to line up at the front entrance with our classes.

On Saturday, we meet at the baseball field to practice with Amy's dad, but sadly, Kathy doesn't show up. Amy practices pitching, and Wendy and I take turns batting. Mr. Keen talks to us like we know what we are doing and seems to think we can do anything. He is full of good advice like, "choke up on the bat," and "keep your eye on the ball." After we hit it, he says, "Run all the way through first base. Never give up and slow down; always run as fast and as hard as you can no matter what." After an hour and a half, we are tired and hungry and decide we've practiced enough. I thank Mr. Keen and walk home.

As I turn the corner to walk down the small alley next to my house, the air surrounding our little back yard smells of roasting hotdogs and flaming charcoal. My heart races; this must mean that Dad came home for the weekend! I pause next to the fence of our yard and see my dad standing above the grill.

"Hi Daddy!" I shout, "You're home!" He looks up at me and his whole face smiles.

"Hey Becky," he says, singing the long *e* in hey and Becky like a song. I run into the backyard through the gate. Dad opens his arms and I collapse on to him, hugging him fiercely. I have not seen him in four long weeks.

I like my hotdogs burned; not completely blackened but with strips of blackness on the sides. Dad knows this, so he roasts my hotdog special for me, keeping it over the charcoal embers longer than everybody else's. However, I have to remind him again that I don't like mustard, and that I can put the ketchup on by myself because I'm 12 now. Our family gathers around our tiny kitchen table. It's made for four, but we squeeze in five, pulling an extra chair from my sister's desk. The table overflows with plates and bowls. We bang elbows and knees, and my left-handed sister keeps bumping my arm causing me to drop my potato chips. I ignore her though, and begin to tell Dad about my baseball tryouts, rambling loudly and quickly while chewing large bites of hotdog. My brother, sister and I are all talking at once. Dad holds up his hand. "Slow down," he says laughing. "One at a time." Mom laughs too and shakes her head. She usually prefers quiet but she seems to enjoy the happy chaos of the moment.

Later that weekend, Vicki, Kris, Mom, Dad and I walk up to the baseball field to practice. Kris pitches to Dad who hits pop flies and grounders to Mom, Vicki and me. Vicki plays on the high school softball team and impresses me with her effortless ability to catch the fly balls that our dad hits in our direction. "Why do girls have to play softball in high school instead of baseball?" I ask her.

"I don't know." She jogs a few steps to the right to catch a ball.

"You can catch a baseball just fine. You don't need a bigger ball."

"I know." She throws the ball back to Kris. "You should go stand over there with Mom." She points across to left field. "I can cover right field."

"He's hitting most of the balls over here, though," I say. My sister rolls her eyes and sighs. I decide to stop asking her about softball and start concentrating on catching. Then, Dad hits a pop fly ball that seems to go up miles and miles. "I got it!" I yell as I keep my eye on the ball and run back and forth. The mayflies swarm around my head, fly up my nose, and then the sun glares in my eyes. "Never mind," I yell getting out of the way. "I don't got it!" The ball hits the ground with a thump. My sister looks at me and shakes her head. We all start laughing.

"You can't say 'I don't got it,'" Vicki says and walks over to pick up the ball. "Besides the fact that it's bad grammar, it's not how you play. You have to at least try and catch the ball not run from it."

"The sun was in my eyes."

"It doesn't matter."

"The mayflies went up my nose."

"Excuses." She says, but she laughs as she throws the ball to Kris.

"Hey Becky," Dad yells. "Come infield a little and I'll hit you some grounders." I move infield where I have a little more luck. "Run up to the ball as it come towards you," my Dad instructs. "Don't wait for it." I run up to the grounders and scoop them up with my glove. Sometimes, I even dive for them. Dad tells me I'm a natural.

Next weekend at tryouts, Amy and I are relieved to see that Kathy's parents let her tryout. Wendy shows up just in time. We huddle together away from the swarm of boys. I glance around at everyone and wonder if they are as nervous as I am.

"Hey Becky!" Mike yells suddenly. "Think fast!"

I turn just in time to see a baseball whizzing towards me. I shoot up my glove and the ball lands inside with a plunk. My glove wobbles on my hand a little, because it's my brother's old one and it's slightly too big.

"Nice." Mike says smiling. I smile back, but hang on to the ball so the girls and I can warm up.

Tommy scowls. "You suck. That was just a lucky catch." I want to punch him in his little pig nose, but instead I shoot him with lasers out of my eyes, making parts of him explode like the aliens in the *Space Invaders* game.

I turn back to the girls, and throw the ball to Amy, who throws it to Kathy, who throws it to Wendy, who throws it back to me. It will be many years before I realize that we are revolutionaries, elbowing our way into the male dominated Waymart Little League. In 1972, the National Organization of Women filed a lawsuit claiming that the Little League organization was discriminating against girls. At the hearings, the Little League's vice president testified about the "physiological differences" between boys and girls. "Girls have weaker bones and muscles than boys," he said, and "dangerously slower reactions times." However, the National Organization of Women won the lawsuit and in December of 1974, President Ford signed a bill opening the Little League baseball program officially to girls. As we warm up, we aren't aware of lawsuits, bills or President Ford. We just want to play baseball.

We are thrilled when all of the girls make teams. Amy and I are assigned to the Dodgers. She is the pitcher, and after a few practices I am declared shortstop. Before our first game, our coach pauses and tells everyone that I am playing shortstop because I hustle and don't stand around and wait for the ball to come to me. He tells them to watch how I quickly stop the ball. I try to play it cool, but inside I feel like Mexican Jumping Beans. I love playing shortstop, but it can be a lot of pressure to remember where I should throw the ball once I stop it.

Our first game is against the Pirates. Before the game, we throw the ball around the infield as Amy warms up on the pitchers mound. "Let's go Becky! Come on Becky!" Dad yells from the stands. I tilt my baseball cap slightly and glance up at the stands to see my dad sitting next to my mom; he is the only spectator clapping and cheering loudly. I catch his eye and put my finger to my lips, but he can't be stopped.

Tommy bats first for the Pirates. He saunters up to the plate, taking a few practice swings as he walks and then locks his eyes on Amy. The infield chants, "Let's go ... come on Amy..." Amy winds up, pitches and Tommy stands still.

"Ball One!" The umpire yells. "Come on Amy ... let's go Amy, Amy..." we sing around the infield. I stand on my tiptoes with my hands on my knees. The weight of my body rests on my toes, and I'm ready to spring forward at a second's notice. Amy winds up again and we start chanting, "Swing batter, batter, batter swing!"

Tommy swings. "Strike one!" The umpire yells and our side of the crowd cheers.

"Come on Amy!" Yells Mike, our second baseman. "Easy out!" I glance toward him and he smiles.

"Let's go Amy!" I yell.

She begins to stare down Tommy. I look up at my dad and he is already clapping. I focus my attention back to Tommy. "Okay," I think to myself. "If the ball comes this way, throw it to first base." Amy pitches the ball and Tommy swings. The ball hits the bat with a loud pop, and I bolt into action running forward unflinchingly with my glove down ready to stop the ball. It bounces into my glove; I grab it and whip it over to first base. Over the cheering crowd I can hear my dad. "Nice stop Becky!" he yells.

We play the Pirates a few more times during the season, but most importantly in the championship game. At the bottom of the ninth inning, Tommy hits a home run with a runner on base and the Pirates beat us by two runs. I am not at that game. My family and I move to Kentucky a week before the playoffs. My moods bounce between the despair of moving and leaving my friends to the joy of having Dad back with our family all of the time.

At the end of baseball season, Kathy mails me my second place trophy with a story cut out from the Wayne County Independent newspaper. It has our names, positions and our team stats. Above the article there's a picture taken after the championship game of the Pirates piled into a lop-sided crazed pyramid each making the number one sign. Tommy lies right in the middle of the pile smiling wildly. There is also a picture of the Dodgers, but Mike is the only one smiling. Amy stands off to the side scowling with her arms folded across her chest. I hang the picture on my bulletin board in my new room. I miss my friends, even Tommy.

The beginning of every baseball season still conjures up the feelings of my childhood, the love of my family, the joy of hanging out with my friends, and the unity of my co-ed Little League team. After that summer, I will always consider everyone to be on the same team, and it will surprise me when I am treated differently because of my gender. I'll fight it when I can. As an adult, I will retain some of the power I felt in sixth grade. In sixth grade, we ruled the school.

Meet My Friend, John Hiller

Tom Stanton

Baseball's best relief pitcher moved into our neighborhood in the spring of 1974.

The news tore through the hormonal halls of Melby Junior High quicker than rumors of foxy Cindy Corbett's break-up. By the end of the school day, everyone knew that John Hiller had taken up residence in Arlington Manor.

The previous year, Hiller had led the American League in games saved, pitched, and finished. He had surrendered a mere run every six innings or so and had struck out nearly a third of the batters he faced. Named both King Tiger and Tiger of the Year, he had finished fourth behind Reggie Jackson, Jim Palmer, and Amos Otis in the league's MVP voting.

And now he was ours.

The apartment complex stood just beyond the school football field, on the other side of a six-foot cyclone fence. From Mrs. Schroeder's math class, you could see its metal-roofed carports and sparse berm of evergreens. It also was where one of my pals, Kevin Daily, lived with his sister and their widowed father.

I had never given much thought to Arlington Manor. It served mostly as a convenient shortcut. On bike or foot, my friends and I weaved through the development to get to the Kmart at Schoenherr and 13 Mile roads or to eat at the restaurant located in its parking lot: Burger Chef, with its pioneering, pickle-rich works bar.

Although it had an in-ground swimming pool, Arlington Manor was nothing special. Its acres of identical-looking, brown-shingled, two-story buildings hardly seemed glorious enough to house the defending American League Fireman of the Year. It didn't look like the kind of place where sports heroes slept. In fact, until John Hiller arrived, no one famous had lived among us.

This was Warren, after all, the largest of Detroit's mostly blue-collar, white-flight suburbs. Our fathers—veterans of World War II and Korea— worked for the auto companies, at the government tank plant, or for the city itself as fire fighters and police officers.

Our subdivision had sprouted from Mr. Stricker's farmland during the early 1960s, hundreds of nearly identical ranch homes with roadside saplings and addresses stenciled on the curbs in black paint. In those years, we played on undeveloped lots amid backhoes, mountains of dirt, and stacks of lumber.

As the city boomed, new schools materialized. Our elementary expanded twice to accommodate the growing families. It carried Robert Frost's name, to inspire us. In actuality, the corny verses of Grandpa Jones on *Hee Haw* would have been more familiar—a road more traveled, you might say—than Frost's poems.

The freshly printed 1974 Tigers yearbook gave John Hiller top billing. He appeared on the first player page, ahead of our baseball trinity, the heroes of '68: Al Kaline, Willie Horton, and Mickey Lolich. Photographed atop the forest-green Detroit dugout, Hiller looked sly and stylish in his Fu Manchu moustache, a fierce bit of cockiness in his eyes.

"A comeback beyond belief," his blurb began.

His spectacular season had followed a lengthy absence from the major leagues. In January 1971, at twenty-seven, Hiller had suffered a heart attack. He missed that entire season and half of the next.

A once heavy smoker, he came back after dropping 55 pounds. He fought doubters on his own club and rose to heights he had never before approached. His amazing return made a compelling story. "John Hiller leads the league in saves—and valor," noted *Sports Illustrated.*

My mom had defied odds, too. At forty-six, she had endured her first brain surgery, to remove a tumor. It left her partially paralyzed on the right side, forcing her to write and paint with her left hand. Medical complications brought more surgeries. Her third came just as Hiller had his heart attack; her sixth the winter he was preparing for his baseball homecoming. Meanwhile, her art pieces—"drip paintings" of finely detailed flower arrangements that ended with rivulets of paint running like tears toward the bottom edge of the frame—were capturing awards as never before.

"Why do you think John Hiller moved here?" I asked my dad. He had been a baseball fan since the 1930s and still talked of the day that "Prince Hal" Newhouser drove around their east-side neighborhood in his showy red car after signing with the Tigers.

"They probably gave him a deal," he said. "They do that sometimes."

Indeed, as it turned out, Hiller wasn't the only Tiger taking up residence two blocks over. Second baseman Gary Sutherland and relief pitcher Luke Walker, both newcomers, moved in as well, and enrolled their children at Frost Elementary. Lance Walker was in my sister Colleen's class.

Sutherland and Walker rated as bonuses in my eyes, the extra fudge on the enormous banana split of John Hiller.

I was 13 that spring, and my life revolved around baseball. When not playing, I scored games on loose-leaf paper to Ernie Harwell and Paul Carey's WJR radio broadcasts. On weekends, I watched the action on color television as George Kell and Larry Osterman tantalized us with inside info. My reading limited itself to the columns of Joe Falls and the articles of Jim Hawkins of the *Free Press*, and, when I could afford them, the current issues of *The Sporting News* and *Baseball Digest*. Spare hours were spent studying the batting averages in the Sunday paper, listening to sports super-fan Ron Cameron on radio, and writing letters to players, everyone from Abbott to Zisk, their envelopes striped with a rainbow of markers.

Baseball was the only thing I excelled at, and I knew it better than anyone at school. Not as an athlete, so much. Though a decent St. Malachy shortstop, I fell short of the best on the field. But when it came to the statistics, history, and trivia of the sport, I took second to no classmate.

Lots of fans followed Hank Aaron's pursuit of Babe Ruth, and many debated whether the Oakland A's qualified as a dynasty after winning two straight championships. And in Michigan thousands could list most every Detroit player who had seen action in the 1972 playoffs when our team, managed by irascible Billy Martin, fell one win shy of the World Series.

But I was the only kid in eighth grade who could explain Wee Willie Keeler's use of the Baltimore Chop in the 1890s or recite the odd-numbered seasons—1921, 1923, 1925, 1927—in which Harry Heilmann had captured a batting title.

I felt destined for baseball greatness. My birth date placed me in a divine lineage. I had been born on December 17. Ty Cobb had debuted on December 18, Kaline on December 19. The presence of John Hiller so close to home confirmed it. It was a harbinger—a crowning anointment.

Hiller presented rich opportunities, and I intended to take full advantage. I imagined getting to know him; playing catch with him outside his apartment; attending games at Tiger Stadium as the guest in his box seats; being hired as the team's batboy based on his recommendation; fielding his post-game phone calls during which I would settle statistical questions for him; convincing him to conduct a pitching clinic for my club; and leading him through the corridors of my school—a public confirmation of my status and significance. Ultimately, I dreamt, he would help clue the Tigers into my surprising passion and stunning potential as a player and clear the way for my eventual signing.

I hung out at Arlington Manor after school. I didn't know specifically where he lived. There were nearly thirty buildings spread across the campus, and each had four to eight units. I moved among them on days when the

Tigers played at home. (Obviously, there was no sense in looking for him during road trips.)

Over the years, I had seen a few other Tigers away from the ballpark. Back-up catcher Jim Price had surfaced at a Little League game one afternoon to watch a friend's son play ball. He stood behind the backstop for several innings and signed autographs. And one evening, Dick McAuliffe, Jim Northrup, and some lesser lights had participated in an off-season benefit basketball game at Carleton Junior High.

But I had never spoken to a player, and that would be required in this case. The way to distinguish myself, I figured, was to tell Hiller about my mom and her surgeries. As someone who had survived a heart attack, he would surely see the connection.

The Hiller stakeout stretched into the summer months. It was frustrating not knowing his car make. Did he drive a Cadillac? Or a Lincoln Continental? Neither turned up. I wasn't alone in this quest. Other kids looked for him, too.

This was the summer of "Bennie and the Jets" and "Band on the Run"— the summer of Nixon's resignation. The Tigers were playing poorly overall, struggling to stay out of last place, and Al Kaline was in his final major league season.

John Hiller pitched well, though not as brilliantly as in 1973. He suffered through a couple rough stretches, including a three-game spell in which he lost two games and allowed six runs and eleven hits in five and two-thirds innings. Still, he got chosen for the All-Star Game.

One afternoon, I was straddling my bike in an Arlington Manor parking lot, hunting for Hiller with two friends when he pulled into a carport directly in front of us.

"That's him, that's him," one stammered.

Hiller emerged from his car in blue jeans. He opened the trunk, packed with brown grocery bags. I was too stunned to speak.

"Mr. Hiller, can we carry your groceries?" my friend asked.

"Sure," he said, his voice more resigned than enthusiastic.

We dumped our bikes in a heap, grabbed his groceries, and trailed him to the apartment building. He opened the door when it buzzed, and we followed him inside. His wife Janis was waiting at the entry with their three children: Wendy, Joey, and Danielle, none older than seven. She looked at us and then at her husband.

"Put 'em on the table," he said.

We set the bags down. I thought he might offer us a Coke and chat for a while. We were gallant young men, having spared him—a heart attack victim—the weighty work of lugging those bags. It seemed the least he could do.

But he never closed the door, and quickly he motioned us toward it.

"Thanks, boys," he said as we left.

We thanked him profusely in chorus from the hallway, calling him "Mr. Hiller" and wishing him good luck as the door shut. For weeks and into the new school year (and even into the decades beyond), we all had stories to tell of our encounter.

Hiller won 17 games that year, and played with the Tigers into 1980 before retiring at 37 as the team's all-time saves leader, a distinction he would hold into the 1990s.

I talked to him one other time—a quarter century later—in 1999 at an old-timers event at Tiger Stadium. My mom had died three years earlier, and I was working on my first baseball memoir, *The Final Season*. I told Hiller the story of carrying his groceries, and he chuckled.

"No shit," he said.

"No shit," I repeated.

We really could have been best friends.

Walk 'Em Home

Victoria Stopp

The ball slammed into my hand and for a moment I thought my bones had exploded. I'd been standing a few feet off second base, staring down the batter with my glove held high. I knew I was in line drive territory, so I always kept my glove in front of my teeth, just in case. It was an act of paranoia that hadn't proven necessary in the many seasons of childhood baseball, but as a college soft baller, the tradition remained.

My team was ahead because I wasn't pitching. We hadn't won a game all season. I was a soccer player and a former baseball player and definitely not a softball stud. As I stood to the left of my base and waited for the clink of bat against ball, I spread my fingers in my dad's old church league glove. There was no padding whatsoever in the palm, just a couple of thin layers of worn leather. My dad taped a circle of moleskin inside to try to cut the sting of a caught ball, but the difference was negligible. I tried to field each ball in the webbing of the glove, avoiding the palm at all costs. My childhood baseball glove was too small for adult softball, and there was no budget for the college to buy us equipment.

Suddenly, the line drive I'd been afraid of, the one that would come straight for my teeth, had arrived, and my decade-old paranoia finally served a purpose. I'd not only protected my face, but I'd caught the ball. I held it in my glove for a second, waiting to figure out if I really had broken every bone in my hand and trying to remember if I'd seen the ball coming at all. I hadn't, I decided. I'd heard it come off the bat but never saw it. I had no idea where it'd been hit until my hand felt like it was on fire.

The college's soccer coach, who'd been in the stands, gave me a high-five as I jogged off the field toward the dugout for an inning change.

"Nice catch," she said, smiling. "But next time, try not to look so surprised that you caught it." I laughed and shook my head like I was in on the joke, but I really hadn't seen the line drive at all.

A month before the ball surprised me in my glove, I sat at a desk on the top floor of the majestic college library, its history and grandiosity lulling me into thoughts of everything except the essay I was supposed to write on the book I was supposed to read. I paced and stared out the window as the rugby team practiced on the field below, intrigued by their violence and humor. I finally turned my attention to the classic in front of me, one of those standards that every undergrad is expected to read. As I forced myself to try to comprehend the highbrow literature, I suddenly sat up and whipped my head around to the window. A familiar sound had jarred me from the doldrums of studying the classics. It was the distinctive ping of metal bat against ball, and I felt the hair rise on my arms and neck.

I jumped up and ran to the larger windows at the back of the library. The softball team was practicing, the rugby team gone, and I'd only read ten pages anyway. I slid my unread books into my backpack and headed for the staircase. I'd never played softball in my life, only baseball, but I thought it couldn't be that much different. *I love college*, I thought, as I descended the stairs after accomplishing nothing.

For anyone who hasn't experienced it, I assure you that the mercy rule shows very little mercy at all. Every time I pitched us to it, which was every time I pitched, we'd been ready to throw down our gloves long before the umpire said "enough." When I'd abandoned my studies in the library and raced down to the field to join the softball team, I had no idea I'd be a pitcher. I imagined myself on second base, loving life like I had as a member of the Comets, my childhood baseball team. But during my first practice, the pitcher announced that her shoulder hurt and she was quitting. We only had one backup pitcher, and our schedule was full of doubleheaders. Our coach asked us all to line up and throw a pitch. I made the mistake of tossing something sort of near the strike zone and was instantly the new backup. If I'd really known what I was getting myself into, I'd have pitched the ball squarely into the dirt during our one-throw tryout.

Midway through our losing season, as I braced myself for one of two unavoidable and oft-repeated things—either I'd throw a perfect strike that would become a home run, or I'd throw another ball and the batter would walk—I pressed my dad's glove to my face and took a deep sniff of the worn leather. As the batter scratched at the red dirt with her cleats and went through her pre-swing ritual, I closed my eyes and smelled the glove again. *How the hell did I get here*, I asked the glove, biting the stitches along its edge like I used to do when I was a nervous Comet. The taste was bitter and dirty and familiar, and I remembered that baseball was fun, and that that's how I'd ended up on a D-III fast-pitch softball field with a smattering of bored fans in the stands.

The Comets rostered the only three girls in what was supposed to be a coed city league. Coach Briscione was ahead of his time, expecting attention and hustle out of everyone regardless of gender. I was proud to be a Comet and wore my oversized, foam-front hat like I'd earned it. Before each Comets game, Coach B called out the starting line up with the authority of a baseball God. The boys and I gathered around him in the dugout as he read from his list, position-by-position and name-by-name, until the last player was called and those of us who'd earned a starting role sprinted onto the field. I always played in my soccer cleats, and I loved the feeling of standing above the dirt on little pegs. I felt tall and important, especially when I was promoted from right field loser (no one ever hit the ball all the way to right field in those days) to starter at second base.

The highlight of my dying baseball career was in the last game of machine pitch league. I was still a Comet, but things were more serious. We were down to two girls in the entire league, both of us with Coach Briscione, and the next year we'd move up to kid pitch. My friend Catherine was far more skilled than I at baseball, so when she suggested I relax my stance, I obeyed. Actually, she said, "why are you standing like that? It looks weird." All season, I'd too literally taken the advice to keep my weight back. I exaggerated my batting stance to look something like a dog peeing, according to Catherine. After her speech, I stood more upright, humiliated but determined, and smacked the first pitch to within inches of going out of the park. As I made it safely to third, I waved to Catherine and wondered how my season would've gone had I stood less like an idiot all year. At 10 years old, I wondered if I'd missed my glory days.

Nine years later, I stood at bat for Agnes Scott College. I was the leadoff hitter for our perpetually losing team, and we were in a game that seemed like we might actually have a chance to win. I remembered Catherine's wisdom from our last machine pitch game. Relax, I told myself, standing tall and grinding my cleats into the batter's box to try to stop my legs from shaking. As the leadoff, I was the litmus test, the royal taster of sorts, for how the opposing team's pitcher would throw. In D-III, we never knew. Some girls were experts, good enough to pitch for a more competitive school. Some were ok, erratic but mostly competent. Some, like me, were downright scary in the circle. I bit down on my cheap mouth guard and wondered why batting helmets didn't come with faceplates.

The first pitch was a beauty. I remembered that feeling of missing my glory days and swung for the fence with a gusto that would've made Catherine and Coach Briscione proud. The ball soared off my bat and landed a few inches from the fence, exactly like it had in that fateful machine pitch game. I made it safely to third, sliding awkwardly like a soccer player because that was the only way I knew how. My teammates went wild, cheering and clapping from the dugout. But as I brushed the clay off my pants, I worried about not hitting a home run, that I'd missed my glory days again, this time at 19. A home run didn't seem like something a mediocre player would get a third shot at, and I tried to smile at the second triple of my not-so-illustrious career. I knew there'd never be another pitch like that—a sitter, hanging in the strike zone as though a machine threw it, begging to be hit into the stands.

We won the game—our only win of the season—but as our coach pulled the team van into the parking lot of Taco Bell, I knew my college career was over. Softball had never felt right, anyway. I missed the comparatively tiny baseballs that actually fit in my hand. I missed Big League Chew bubblegum and Topps cards and seeing friends in the stands. Mostly, I missed baseball and Coach Briscione. Suffering through another season as an untalented pitcher wouldn't bring forth another chance at glory. Even on the heels of our big win, the truth was as apparent as the bruise on my palm. I sighed and thought of post-game pizza binges with my Comets friends. The college's $5-per-player allotment bought me nachos and a Pepsi, and I pocketed the change, smiling and telling myself I'd just gotten paid to play ball, and that surely there was nothing more glorious than that.

The Language of the Gods

BRENDAN O'MEARA

> "The sounds of the game are really kind of cool, something
> that doesn't get talked about a lot… they really do resonate.
> Everybody really remembers sounds."
> —P.J. Pilittere, hitting coach
> for the Trenton Thunder[1]

You don't need eyes to know if a ball traveled 450 feet, just a keen set of
ears and a sense of wonder.

People often talk about the sounds of the game of baseball in *Field-of-
Dreamy* terms: crack of the bat, ball on glove, sliding into second, etc. These
are lower-case sounds. I'm talking Sounds, even *smells*, sensory inputs that
made Peter Gammons, the famed baseball writer, say that Ted Williams, Don
Mattingly and Mark McGuire spoke the "language of the gods."[2]

I remember an anecdote around the 1999 All-Star Game, the one at Fenway Park, the one Williams was toured around in his wheelchair. When someone finally parked him in the center of the diamond, the best players of the
day huddled around the man many called the greatest hitter that ever lived,
like he was God. Williams pulled McGuire down to his level. McGuire had
just come off his record-setting—though andro-enhanced—seventy-home-
run season for the Cardinals. Williams asked him, "Have you ever smelled
the bat burning?"[3]

McGuire, happy that Williams even knew who he was, said he had.

It's the perfect confluence of elite power-on-power. A no-name-taking,
four-seam fastball must whip in with a little bit of rise. It should scream in
somewhere north of 95 mph, but this isn't an exact science. Next, a batter
with world-shaking bat speed—someone like McGuire—must make contact
and foul the ball straight back to the screen. It's the firmest, most aggressive
contact you can make without hitting the ball to the deepest, most remote

recesses of a ballpark. It's impossibly frustrating to be that close to such contact, but if struck just right, the seams burn the wood.

"Only the guys who whip that lumber have smelled it," Williams said.[4]

* * *

I always wanted to call malarkey when I heard that. But who was I? My career ended with a whimper in the hallways of UMass Amherst, cut in my sophomore year. I had come across several ballplayers I might call "elite." While in high school, I remember standing at my native shortstop when one of the opposing players hit a ball my way. The ball sounded like a bottle rocket as it approached, this beautiful, liquid hiss. I could barely regain my bearings to throw the ball because I'd never heard anything come off the bat like that.[5]

Late in the summer when the heat's edge dulls, the leaves start to turn, and the best teams gear up for the playoffs, I decided to put this Sound of the Game to the test. I used to live five miles from where the Trenton Thunder, a AA affiliate of the New York Yankees, call home.

I sent an electronic mail to the Sports Information Director (SID) wondering if I may catch batting practice and maybe speak to the hitting coach. I looked up the coach: P.J. Pilittere. He had a modest career in the minors, reaching AAA-ball. He has the sturdy fullback-build you expect in a catcher: broad shoulders, the brick-wall torso of a backstop and his energy for all things hitting and baseball is childishly charming. Few people use words like "inertia," "kinetic chain," and "nasty hammer" with such glee.

When I first arrived at the ballpark on a quiet pre-game afternoon in early September, I took sight of the surrounding ephemera, banners and signage waiting for storage. At Arm & Hammer Park, you're first struck by flags with Derek Jeter, David Eckstein, and Chase the Bat Dog.

Jeter's time at Trenton was relegated to a rehab start, but the Trenton Thunder sees fit to boast his presence. Minor League baseball is all about reaching the next level, and selling Minor League baseball to fans makes use of this kind of curriculum vitae: look who played here! Maybe you'll see the next Jeter out there today!

SID responds quickly to my text message and coaxes me into the ballpark. Arm & Hammer Park is so empty, like a church before mass. We stand in the press box, which is a line of chairs at a counter overlooking the field about fifteen-to-twenty feet in height above home plate and one hundred feet behind, give or take. Were it not for the backstop, a wicked wood-burning (so I'm led to believe) foul tip could whip straight back and knock out a MacBook Pro.

SID, who also moonlights as a broadcaster for the team while substitute teaching in the area schools[6] is in his late 20s and if he hasn't "made it" by the time he's 31, he's finding a new line of work. He knows what a drag journalism can be and he's had about enough. You can see the sullen look in his eyes, but he perks up when he talks about the team, namely Dustin Fowler, a young, physically unassuming lefty, who is known to hit the ever-living shit out of every pitch that comes his way. SID looks out onto the field.

"We don't have practice jerseys with last names, but Fowler's about 5-foot-10-inches, a lefty, can *run* and doesn't look like a power guy. He hit a ball the other night that went over the light tower in right field," SID says, nearly needing to wipe the drool off his freshly shaven chin. "You'll *know* when he hits the ball."

The American flag out in center field blows from left to right at a gentle pace. It's what you might call a perfect day to be at the ballpark. Batting practice will start soon, but in the meantime, I look around the stadium to see more banners of former players: Andrew Brackman, Chase the Bat Dog and Derby, Chase's younger successor to the mantle.

A keg of baseballs gets wheeled out to the mound about 30 feet from home plate. The pitcher will stand behind the L-screen so as to avoid death. Keeping the distance this short allows this pitcher to throw hundreds of pitches while not straining the ol' rotator cuff too much. He can throw relatively easy, and the ball will still arrive at the batter in a time that won't completely fudge with his timing when the opposing pitcher takes to the hill from 66-feet 6-inches away.

There are a few lefties who seem to match the build of SID's description of Dustin Fowler. One steps in and takes a crack at the pitch and it makes that nice crisp sound you want to hear. I wouldn't call it explosive, but it isn't pedestrian either. This has become my frame of reference seeing as, you know, *all* these guys are pro players with most still eyeing the possibility of cracking a Big League roster.

Here each player gets six pitches before switching out. They'll rotate through about five times, each getting somewhere around thirty total swings. The six at a time keeps the focus sharp and everyone limber and free from boredom.

Round after round comes through the cages. A few of the guys put some hefty charges into the ball finding the gaps or the gaggle of pitchers who found the one 100-square-foot area of shade way out in right center. There they gather like grazing cattle.

The final group of batters enters the cage. By this point my ears had been numbed to the respectable crack of the AA hitters. The next batter approaches the plate and taps it with his lumber. I mean, it's all well and good and I heard nothing that was all that memorable. The pitcher delivers.

In fact they're making contact that I once…

Whaaaaaaaaat the hell was thaaaaaaaat?!

…made myself. Nope. Not even close.

That ball left the ballpark on a truly terrifying vector and the sound[7] of the bat was nothing like I had ever heard before *this* close to the field. His hands were high, loose, just over his right shoulder ready to launch as the next pitch came in and…

Whaaaaaaaaaat is the meaning of this?!

The next bit of violent contact may have stayed 10 feet above the ground yet had enough sheer mass × acceleration—which is to say Newtonian force[8]—behind it that it cleared the fence a foot over the 330 number on the right field corner, right above the Peace of Mind Bank of Choice advertisement.

He proceeds to hit another three balls out of the park *in the first round* of BP.

This is Dustin Fowler.

Fowler has a gentle rock to his lower body, something limber, like fine architecture that moves with the gentle pulsations of the earth. As the pitcher brings the ball up to his right ear, Fowler begins to load the spring: He shifts a quorum of mass onto his back leg as he steps forward with his right foot starting to move his weight through the moment of impact. At this point, the back leg punches his hips through the pitch as he clears his iliac and opens it toward the Delaware River 100 yards clear of that formality of a fence in right field. By this point, the hands, up over his left shoulder[9] supple, on a swivel, sense the impeding recruitment from the lower body and drop down on a forty-five-degree angle—the better to chop through the ball and reverse its pitcher-delivered topspin/sidespin and impart his own anti-spin—which is to say backspin to give the ball the proper…

Oh My Gaaaaaaaaaaawd! When will it land!?

…lift, the proper lift, to send that motherfucker from home plate to where nobody—and I mean *nobody*—shagging balls even moves as the ball nearly takes out a light bulb on the 100-foot tall light tower 350 feet from home plate and yet the ball keeps going and vanishes into an unassuming, deciduous tree beyond the fence.

And his swing looks so easy[10] not like former MLB greats like Gary Sheffield and Barry Bonds, whose swings were so violent they needed a state-issued permit to carry such a firearm.

Fowler sort of waddles out of the cage like a penguin leans against the bat and stands in the on deck circle watching his other teammates hit the ball. It's hard to even classify what the others do as hitting after watching Fowler go nuclear on about 20 of the 30 pitches he saw. Fowler then scratches his rear end. Puts down his helmet. Leaves the field.

All the while, standing with his lumberjack forearms on the cage, was P.J. Pilittere, the conductor of this symphony of sound.

*   *   *

Pilittere remembers a time when he was about eight years old, going to the 1989 All-Star Game at Anaheim Stadium. He and his dad were walking along the stands in right field, near the foul pole where the bullpen was. They sat down and Pilittere heard this explosion, this eruption. He told me, "'Dad, what is that? Is that a car backfiring?'" The two looked down into the bullpen, and it was Nolan Ryan, in his eighth and final All-Star Game, warming up. This was the Nolan Ryan who had already been in the league for 23 years and he still generated some serious vinegar.

Pilittere told me, "So that sound for me as an eight-year-old catcher, that put me through the roof. I want to make that sound. You know what I mean? THAT part of the glove is where you get it from."

He ran into his office and grabbed his catcher's mitt, put it on his hand, and punched it.

He pointed to that part of the mitt that corresponds directly to the terminal end of the second and third metacarpals, the part that will, over time, get increasingly calcified by receiving grenades from pitchers of Ryan's ilk. "But to hear that noise..." Pilittere told me, "I can still hear that noise right now standing here talking to you. That's how loud it was and how resonating it was and I think that put me over the edge. You know what I mean?"

He also said some pitchers create such whip on the ball that their fingers sound like Velcro coming off the seams.

And Pilittere said that catching the ball there just south of the webbing, thus eliciting that BANG!, is an ear worm for the hitter. It gets in the hitter's head. As if the humming-bird hiss of the ball wasn't enough, that explosion in the mitt can add 5 mph to the ball in a hitter's head, make the pitcher seem like he's throwing faster, make you think you have to gear your swing up that much sooner, and maybe force the hitter out on the front foot of a nasty *chonge* (sic), and flutter a ball behind third base or miss it entirely

So I had to ask him about this "language of the gods." Is it true that the wood burns if a hitter fouls a ball straight back?

Pilittere contended that *he* never had quite the bat speed to smell it off his own bat, but he knows it's true and here's the kicker: If a guy fouls one back—I mean a real screamer that would seem to tear the backstop a new one—guys will put the barrel of the bat right up to their face. "They're smelling the burning wood," Pilittere told me, "which is habit for some guys, superstition for some guys. It's a pretty cool smell."

It must be. It must be nice to be bilingual in English and the language of the gods.

*   *   *

Not more than two weeks later, my wife and I went to a game between the hapless Marlins and the equally hapless Phillies at Citizens Bank Park.[11]

We went early so we could see batting practice and maybe catch a home run ball for a five-ounce keepsake. Giancarlo Stanton, the Marlins slugger and $315 *million* man, would be taking BP.

Stanton made a reputation for hitting the ball not just far, but perilously far, with exit velocity north of 100 mph.[12] He's a video game in real life. He's also six-foot-six inches tall and 245 pounds, throws right, bats right, plays right field. His body has the bulging musculature of an Adonis. Honestly, he doesn't belong on a baseball field; he belongs in a museum.

He took hold of his bat and stood in the cage. He looked comically large, too much like Thor, and the first ball he swung at hit the L-screen. I nearly came out of my shoes. The ball triggered the most jarring, most electric, most sonically charged bout of contact I have ever heard. *And I was standing 329 feet away in the front row of the outfield bleachers.* This being the first round, he was hitting the ball up the middle and to right field and the speed of the ball was cartoonish in its velocity. The sound *echoed* after contact, this in a place of 1.15 million square feet.[13]

By the time he started pulling the ball to the left field alley, an army of people came to the left field bleachers because it was inevitable that he'd hit balls that would reach us in about 2.8 seconds after impact.

And while I never caught a ball, they flew out with near lunar predictability, to the upper deck overhead. Time after time, Stanton's contact was what P.J. Pilittere tries to coach out of players, players like Dustin Fowler.

Stanton put on a symphonic clinic of hitting. Each time he swung, we braced for impact.

One person standing a few rows behind me said to his friend after Stanton crushed a ball, "It *sounds* different, doesn't it?"

I looked at my wife. She looked at me.

Then the man a few rows back added, "That's just stupid."

NOTES

1. P.J. Pilittere (Thunder hitting coach), interview with author, September 2016.

2. Gammons, Peter, "Can You Smell the Bat Burning?" ESPN.com, July 5, 1999. http://www.espn.com/gammons/s/2002/0705/1402438.html

3. *Ibid.*

4. *Ibid.*

5. Taking one of these suckers off the chest, shin, or nethers is one of the more memorable experiences you'll have as a ballplayer. Nothing like seeing the stitches of the ball imprint on the tibia.

6. Adam Giardino (Thunder SID), interview with author, September 2016.

7. P.J. says, "That's exciting from a coaching perspective. Say you have someone that can make that sound, those are the guys we need to really lock into. You try to find as many of those guys that can produce that sound as possible. And your job as coaches is to make

that sound come out more. You know what I mean? Once they make that sound come out more consistently, then we've got a Major League player. You know what I mean?"

8. P.J. says, "It's really neat as a coach because I know there's things mechanically we can do to make swings more efficient and shorter to produce louder sounds, to produce higher exit velocities, to produce more base hits."

9. P.J. says, "I was having a conversation with Fowler last week about it. 'Think of where you were last year and think about how much shorter your swing is now. Think about the results and the success you've had this year. They go hand in hand.' From a sonic perspective, that's the job. To get it cleaned up and get that thing really humming in there."

10. P.J. says, "Getting into a loaded position early enough so I can take my bat straight to the baseball with no wasted movement. Guys you see who have this loop to their swing and start hitting the ball this way, or guys that start to lose their hands way form their body. A guy like Dustin, for example, he'll be in this position and he'll get to touchdown and he will be directly to the ball. Bang. Bang. Short, no wasted movement, no wasted inertia; some people will say you're not breaking the kinetic chain. It's boom. Boom. I don't like to talk about it like that. That's a little much at times. But we think of it as short. Direct. Simple. A. B. My hands are A. Baseball is B. I gotta get there fast. I think an easy, simple way to describe it is you're not going to produce that *sound* that you're looking for by being strong. If I can get from A to B with speed—fast and quick—that's going to produce that loud, loud noise."

11. I dearly hoped some monster would foul one back so hard that he would smell his bat, but it never happened.

12. https://en.wikipedia.org/wiki/Giancarlo_Stanton

13. http://philadelphia.phillies.mlb.com/phi/ballpark/information/index.jsp?content=facts_figures

PART II

The Season

It's gritty. It's long. It's not like that wimpy handful of games they play in the NFL. The baseball season is a serious haul. There aren't many days off and there's plenty of travel. We baseball fans can only imagine the grind. April through September—maybe October, too, if we're lucky. And for us spectators, it's usually a roller coaster. You're up in April only to be down in May. The mid-season feels like it could be a turning point. That end-of-season rally is either glorious or heartbreaking.

We get our chances to go to some, or many, games. We commiserate. We wear our gear and fly our flags and sometimes, if we're lucky, plan our summer schedules around our favorite teams' schedules.

No one is out of the running in the beginning of the season. A rally is always possible after the All-Star break. Individual accomplishments can be cheered the whole season through. It is the greatest, real-time narrative in history.

The Ten Commandments
of a Baseball Fan
(As Taught to Me by My Wife)

HENRY DOSS

As a young man, I was never into baseball. My upbringing was a bit ...
let's go with "unsophisticated." As a consequence of this, my athletic interests
ran more toward shooting (pool), lifting (beer cans), and running (from the
truant officer). Baseball, requiring as it did talents like showing up at a specific
time, some marginal situational awareness, and at least a little coordination,
was just not in the cards for me. So I just never got into it, never watched it
on TV, never had "my team," never went to a game (not of any kind, ever)
and in general lived a life wholly and totally unaware of the game.

This state of affairs remained constant for me until I married someone
who is not so much a baseball fan as a baseball idolater, bordering on the
fanatic, and intolerant of the absence of enthusiasm for the game. (There is
a shrine in our home; it is where she keeps her 1984, Games 3, 4 and 5, World
Series tickets, pennant, and program. It is a holy place.)

My unawareness of and lack of appreciation for the game of baseball
was clearly something that was not going to last, insofar as I wished to live
in the homes we built, drive the cars we shared, eat the food we bought, or
participate in any reasonable manner in a shared life. Let me try to be a little
clearer, just in case this sounds flippant. Not being at the very least an informed
and frequent participant in the baseball world was **required** in my marriage.
Moreover, it was just kind of assumed, as you would assume that breathing
would be a part of our marriage. How can you live without breathing? By the
same token, how can you live and be married (at least to my wife) without
being a baseball fan? (Don't try "false analogy" arguments here. Let me save
you some time. Won't work.)

40

I chose to become a willing participant in my wife's infatuation. And while it's still true that I would probably not, on my own, be a big fan of baseball, I have become a minor authority, and possess a minor-level of participatory skill in the sport, simply by being "willing." And I get to live here, too. So, as a result of my willingness to be a participant in her sport, I've accumulated decades of knowledge (just a bit), game experiences, (most fun, some really cool), and even at ideal times of the season, a budding appreciation for just what baseball can be.

To illustrate this, and to better illustrate her level of commitment to this game, I found myself at the 2016 Annual Mayo Smith Society luncheon in Detroit—a ten-hour drive from our home—listening to Mickey Lolich hold forth on the ins-and-outs of using (or, in his judgment, not using) the modern pitch count strategy; and I found myself enjoying, appreciating, and even kind of understanding what he was talking about. On our drive back home from this event, we got to talking about "how to be a baseball fan," and it occurred to me that over the years, I have been schooled in the Ten Commandments of a Baseball Fan, according to my wife. And, without actually thinking about it, I have come to a place where I observe these Commandments almost automatically, without even thinking. They are, like all Commandments, the distilled essence of what it means to *be* something; and so, for any and all who might struggle to understand the ethical dimension of being a true fan of baseball, and who aspire to being an apprentice, I share these Ten Commandments for your edification.

The Ten Commandments of a Baseball Fan

1. You never, ever leave a game until it is over. This is the Supreme Commandment. The Prime Directive. It is the Commandment of Commandments. You. Do. Not. Violate. This. I have been at games that were absolutely, positively hopeless, in bad weather, the stands emptying, the announcers bored, the team dispirited. I have occasionally at times like this suggested, ever so gently, that maybe we could "get a head start on traffic." At best, I get a sideways glimpse of disgust. You are there to see the game, and see the game you will to the last damn pitch.

2. You never, ever give up on your team. (See the Prime Directive, above.) At some point in a bad season, any reasonable person will simply give up on post-season hopes. Do the math and it tells you: "Game over." But the Commandment says: "There is always hope. The math only tells you what is likely, not what is decided. And when your team is at the bottom of the standings, and everything seems to be going wrong, and the disloyal are jumping ship, you stand firm. It's never too soon to pull out the Wild

Card argument. And when the math tells you something that even the most fanatically loyal can't ignore, then the conversation goes to building for next year, along with some really good, strong arguments for why the middle relievers were the problem all along, but other than that we played really, really well, probably better than any other team, so in some way, were it not for this little pitching problem we'd be right in there for the playoffs, so it's not "us" that is losing, it's one or two middle relievers who under-performed, so, clearly, we really have the best team in major league baseball and should be going to the post-season or for **DAMN SURE WE WILL NEXT YEAR!** (**Bonus Note:** Never, I mean never, disagree with these arguments. Nod sagely, wrinkle your brow as if processing, harrumph ever so slightly and then say gently, "You know, I think you're right.")

3. **Honor MLB TV. Use it.** MLB TV must be recognized as the greatest invention of all time. With it you are never, ever out of range of listening to, watching or "reading" a game. (Note: Some of the MLB game coverage can be understood almost as "reading" the game as it goes. Just in case you're curious.) This must be taken as a given, a foundational assumption to your life, because there is a corollary Commandment to honoring MLB TV. That is that you must use it all the time. It is not enough that it's there. It must be used. For every game, all the time, no matter what. So, you're at the dentist? Use your headphones and listen. Doing yard work? Same thing. Driving? Bluetooth the game into your car system. Walking? Listen while you walk. Whatever. The thing to remember is that during baseball season, MLB TV must be on, and you must be attending to it. Always.

4. **Honor the IPad, for it gives us magic access to games.** Most of you will not know this, but the IPad was invented solely for the purpose of watching baseball. All of the other uses we have found for it are incidental to its primary function as a means of watching baseball. Even less well known is the fact that it was specially designed for watching games in bed. While your spouse sleeps (or tries to sleep.) Both the volume and the screen brightness are carefully engineered to provide maximum wakefulness, so you will not be interrupted by sleep. This has the added bonus of making your spouse grateful for helping him to stay awake, too. So, HONOR THE DAMN IPAD!

5. **Find a ballpark near to where you are traveling. Go.** Geographers, geometrists, cartographers, and satellite imagery … they all lie. There is always, without exception, a ballpark nearby to wherever you happen to be traveling, and it is a violation of this Commandment if you don't include a ball game in your itinerary. Work is important, yes. But bypassing the chance to go to a game is a sin. Don't do it.

Now some of you may dispute this, but that would be because you don't understand baseball geometry according to Euclid. There is a little-known, little-studied axiom of Euclid's that makes what is known as the "Spherical Boundary Exception." It basically says that all of the axioms (things like space, and straight lines and angles and stuff) apply to all spatial phenomena *except in the presence of a spherical shape that is precisely the shape and size of a baseball.* When a baseball is present, space bends to accommodate the needs of true fans, and what might seem a great distance becomes, in fact, a short distance. (If you don't believe this, the detailed proof is in *Conics*. Look it up!) What this means for observing the Commandments is this: *There is always a baseball stadium near where you are going. Always. No exceptions.* For example, if you are going to the Central or Western United States you would, of course, drop by St. Louis to visit the Cardinals at their home stadium. So, the next time you're traveling to, say, South Dakota, and your spouse says "Why don't we go to St. Louis for a game while we're 'out there'?" just nod and say yes, and trust Euclid to make it OK.

6. Spring Training is a mandatory pilgrimage, preferably an annual one. There are things you want to do, things you'd like to do and things that are on your list to do "someday." Spring Training falls into the Commandment category as something that "must be done." In fact, it is not something to be done because it is fun, but because, well, it must be done. Spring Training is the initiation rite, the passage from unwashed to serious fan. The Commandment is to simply go. No more need be said.

7. Buy all baseball paraphernalia. There is no ethical, moral, financial or practical limit to the amount of baseball paraphernalia you can (should!) buy. There is no such thing as redundant T-shirts, sweatshirts, pants, hats, flags, doodads, kitsch, stuff. There is an infinite array of baseball paraphernalia you can own. Books, bobble heads, banners, baseballs. And that's only a partial list of just the "B's"! If you are a real fan, you simply buy the stuff. Walking into the park for a game, you would no more wonder whether or not to buy a program than you would wonder whether or not to buy two hot dogs between the third and fourth innings. The Commandment says, "buy!" and so buy you must. As a corollary, some true believers will extend this Commandment to include "Display this crap all over the house everywhere." I take no personal position on the question of "display" with respect to "buy," leaving doctrinal disputes of this level of complexity to my superiors. But I do know that some things (see reference to 1984 World Series tickets, above) move beyond the level of "stuff" to a much more sacrosanct state of being. So, buy, for damn sure; display as your heart (and your spouse) suggest.

8. Anyone who is a baseball fan is OK. No exceptions. If you are a serious baseball fan—really, really a serious fan—you are by definition an

OK sort of person. You might have some faults—drunkenness, profligacy, unsavory character, whatever. But as a baseball fan, these will all be considered "minor character flaws" because if you love baseball (and you follow the Commandments) then there simply must be a good reason for your faults.

Here's an example. My wife is what you might call a "liberal." She has a limited tolerance for conservative ideology. We were at a game in Baltimore one night. I looked behind me and saw someone I thought I recognized. I asked her "Is that George Will?" I thought for sure I'd elicit a minor tirade about conservative politics. She turned around and looked. She said: "Yeah. Man he's a great baseball writer. One of the best." And that was it. Baseball fan? You're OK.

9. Thou Must Eat Your Peanuts with the Shell On: This Commandment is a bit obscure, and I'm not personally sure where it comes from, why it's important or just what the hell purpose it serves. But, then, I don't write the Commandments. But if you intend to be a baseball fan, you must observe: There is one and only one way to eat peanuts at a ballpark, and that is whole, with the shell still on. You take the peanut out of the bag and you shove it in your face and you chew. That's it. It is not our place to question the wisdom of these kinds of Commandments, but simply to follow them. Does wonders for your digestion, too.

10. It is OK to root for a team other than your favorite in postseason play, when your "chosen team" has been eliminated. Inevitably, the law of averages will tell you that your team will not be in every postseason, and certainly not in every World Series. So, every fan comes to a point when their team is out, and they either watch the entire post-season passively or make a "temporary adoption" of a favorite post-season team. This is a painful process, and lacks clarity. How you choose which teams to have as second, third, or fourth choices is a mystery, known only to a few. In our house it goes: Tigers, Pirates, Nationals, Orioles. There are clues to how this chain of loyalty evolved, but it's surrounded by a world of unspoken negotiation and vague geography. However it might actually work, the Commandment allows this temporary shift of loyalty to ensure the fan has the opportunity to enjoy the entirety of the season (see Commandments 2, 3, 4, 5 and 7 for why this so).

However, amongst the Initiates there is a non–Canonical corollary to this second, third and fourth choice commandment. That corollary is that you do not, ever, have a fifth pick. Having a fifth pick is the equivalent of entering the 9th Circle of Baseball Hell, named by Dante as the "Wholly and Totally Lost Fan" circle. It is inhabited by sad, defeated baseball fans, doomed for all eternity to watch replays of inconsequential games, played by teams they don't care about, on fuzzy screens, with bad sound, wearing a logo-less, nondescript, generic baseball cap. Don't do this.

For the reluctant baseball fan, the accidental fan, the learning process is different from that of the true fan. The true fan just absorbs truth left and right. The reluctant fan has to be told, instructed. What comes easily to the natural fan comes as lessons to the accidental fan. The Ten Commandments of a Baseball Fan will help you keep your behavior and thinking in line with expectations, and will help you to avoid conflict. So, the next time you are crushing your head under the pillow, trying to sleep, while some extra-inning game on the opposite coast from you is blaring on MLB TV, and you have just paid the credit card bill that had $3,457 worth of baseball crap on it, and you are going over and over in your own head just how it is that Cincinnati is somehow close to the meeting you have the next week in Atlanta (so why not go to a game in Cincinnati!?!?!?), and … well, you get the picture. The next time this happens, just take a deep breath, enjoy the baseball and be glad for Commandment 8. Because without it, you might be in trouble.

The Girl from Cleveland

NANCY A. GUTIERREZ

One summer's evening, when I was in high school, I remember pacing up and down my kitchen when a Cleveland Indians pitcher was working on a no-hitter. A few clicks on the keyboard, as I write this essay, and I discover that the date must have been June 10, 1966, and the pitcher was Sonny Siebert. The kitchen was only half-lit, as only one soft bulb was on over the sink, and the windows were open, so I could hear the summer evening sounds of the neighborhood and feel the cooling of the night. My parents were around somewhere, I think out on the front porch, and my younger brothers were also absent, out in the neighborhood doing whatever boys do. So the house was quiet and I was the only one paying attention to this historic event. I had my transistor radio up to my ear and waiting for each pitch was unbearable, tortuous, excruciating. The sound of the game over the radio—there is nothing so distinctive as the sounds that one hears during a radio broadcast of a night baseball game—tormented me: silence but not silence, as 10,469 murmuring and anxious fans tried not to jinx a wondrous feat and the announcers maintained a tense patter and gingerly avoided saying "no-hitter." Siebert won the game, allowing only two men on base. Even now, 50 years later, the experience is as vivid to me as if it were yesterday.

If I drill down on exactly what this experience is, it is the waiting between each pitch. I remember holding my breath and letting it out; I remember the excitement before and after each pitch and after each out. Often you hear people say that this waiting slows down the game. The opposite is true, as any fan of the game realizes. The *in-between* each pitch is where the tension and excitement lay, for that is when the pitcher assesses the context—the batter's talents and history, the ball count, the inning, the number of men on base, the number of outs—and determines the perfect pitch that will paralyze his opponent. And that is where the fan imagines the next move in the arc of the game.

46

The writer, John Gardner, once compared the experience of reading to "a vivid and continuous dream." So, too, is the experience of a baseball game. But not a dream in the sense of something just at the edge of our consciousness, romantic and quixotic—but rather, a dream that moves, inexorably and inevitably, as each step leads to a next step, to a denouement that has its own logic and lucidity. The experience of immersing oneself in a baseball game is to inhabit a world parallel to our own, proceeding apace with its own rationale and inevitability. In other words, it is a story. If it is the space between pitches that constitutes our connection to the game, then it's arguable that defense, not offense is the imaginative nexus.

*   *   *

In the fall of 1963, three years before Seibert's no-hitter, I was a seventh-grader, attending a parochial school, not one of the popular girls, a bit nerdy, with baby blue glasses (this last data point should be a clear signal why I was not one of the popular girls). I lived in Cleveland Heights, Ohio, one of the older suburbs in Cleveland, and I *knew* this was one of the most boring places in the world. And how did I know this? By reading.

I loved to read. Many book lovers will tell you that they are indiscriminate readers—that they will read anything and everything. Not me. I was picky. While, by the time I was 12, I had persuaded my parents to approve my getting an adult library card, so I could take out 10 books a week from either the children's or adult's section, I would only read books about girls. And for a very long time, I would only read stories written in the third person. No first-person narratives for me. I can't tell you why, but I can tell you that the book that broke this barrier was Mary Stewart's *This Rough Magic* (1964), which I found in my Aunt Dian's home, when I was desperate for something to read to take me away from her kids. Greece was the locale of this novel, not Cleveland Heights.

Into this world, came Sister Mary Judith, my seventh-grade teacher and a Pittsburgh Pirates fan (her mother order, the Felician Sisters, was head-quartered in Pittsburgh). Sister Judith was so much a baseball fan that she persuaded the parents of one of the students in our class to bring a portable television to our classroom to watch the World Series in the fall of 1963. Since I was a dutiful and impressionable student, I took this break in the classroom routine as something meaningful and noteworthy. Then, in the spring, Sister Judith played a further role in my pathway to becoming a baseball fan. Every year the Cleveland newspaper, the *Plain Dealer,* offered free Cleveland Indians baseball tickets to students who made straight A's in the fourth quarter: one pair to students in grades 4–6, *seven* pair to *seven* different games to students in grades 7–12. (This promotion has long been discontinued. We will never know how many baseball fans were created—or how many children were motivated to excel academically—as a result of this generous and prescient publicity campaign). Come spring 1964, Sister Judith actively promoted this perk, and I proudly took my report card to the *Plain Dealer* offices, at the bottom of East 9th Street, and received my seven pair of tickets to attend seven (seven!) baseball games.

At the time, the Cleveland Indians were one of 10 teams in the American League. This is the era before divisions and playoffs. The team with the most wins in the American League met the team with the most wins in the National League, in early October, to determine the winner of the World Series. Cleveland was at the beginning of a three-and-a-half decade run of mediocrity, but no one knew that yet. The 1950s had been good years, but the Indians had the misfortune to be the second-best team in the League next to the Yankees of Mantle, Berra, Ford, and Rizzuto. And the Yankees run, of course, followed the 1954 World Series, when the Indians lost, 0–4, to the Giants and their rookie super star, Willie Mays.

I was not particularly interested in sports, and it would be more than 10 years before Title IX took hold in the schools to provide real opportunities for team sports for girls. However, it was clear to me pretty quickly in 1963, that going to the baseball games would be anticlimactic, unless I knew something about the game and the players. So, I began to read the *Plain Dealer* and to follow the Tribe. But while Sister Judith and the free tickets clearly are a piece of the story, they are not the only important pieces.

Reading.

* * *

Somehow into this space came Duane Decker, whose baseball novels about the fictional Major League Blue Sox team became my primer. If you Google Decker, you will find numerous accolades about his stories. Each novel focuses on one position player and tells the story of how that position player came to be a regular on the team. Each book was the chronicle of a season. Decker wrote thirteen books in all, nine books focusing on the first team and the next several on the next generation. Unfortunately, he did not complete the second generation. The stories are formulaic, of course: while each fictional player has talent, some more than others, what makes each successful is an ineffable quality that goes beyond innate ability: persistence or hard work or being a team player or giving the game your all. The formula works, as the narrative arc is authentic and believable.

But equal in importance to this growth-of-the-hero formula is Decker's understanding of the *game* of baseball. His protagonists, as I said above, were position players, so each book offered a clinic on playing the particular position in the field. Here is where I learned that a ball hit over the third baseman's head is the shortstop's ball. Here is where I learned that the most difficult defense in baseball is when runners are on second and third, with one out. Here is where I learned about the infield fly rule, the importance of the cutoff man, the ineffable beauty of the sacrifice bunt, the mind game between a man on first and the pitcher.

Duane Decker brought me into the community of baseball readers, teaching me the grammar of the myth. I gravitated to this game as I already was a lover of narrative, and watching baseball—watching how the defense was set up and seeing whether or not it worked—was a delicious and tangible variation of this experience. The immediacy within each game fascinated me with its shifting plotlines. And the assorted rituals grounded each game in an historical continuum. I loved it. It was suspense. It was story.

The archetypal battle between batter and pitcher is often posed as the dominant American plotline—think of *The Natural* or "Casey at the Bat," for example. But another, perhaps more stirring although less flamboyant, story is told in the periphery, just sideways from the two men at the center of the action, as each fielder positions himself in relation to the batter, but not only where the batter stands, but also in relation to how the position player understands the batter's offensive history, the immediate context of the game, and the abilities of his fellow fielders. The storyline advances, informed not only as pitch follows pitch, but also by the changing count and the reactive moves of the fielders: the second baseman moving to second base to hold the runner in place; the third baseman running in to the plate, as the pitcher releases the ball, to field a possible bunt; the left fielder playing in, to be able to make a throw to the plate, in the event of a fly ball. Experienced readers of the game—i.e. baseball fans—instinctively expect such moves and applaud when a player demonstrates this intuitive skill by anticipating where the ball is hit or boo their displeasure when a player falls short.

As the balls and strikes are called, the players shift themselves on the field. What do we call these maneuvers? A dance? A poem? "Call-and-response"?

All of these, of course. It is a narrative that we read.

But in retrospect, I can add another aspect that was not evident to me at the time. For the most part in the early and mid–1960s, sport was a domain that was closed to girls and women. As I mentioned earlier, Title IX was well in the future. The demands of being a proficient baseball reader—a reader who understands offense and defense—these demands are easily met by girls. In fact, as we know, girls in general are much better readers than boys, at least until boys catch up in their late teens. I would argue that, for girls of my generation, the pathway to becoming a fan was through our adeptness in reading.

I was not alone in my love of baseball and the Indians. I entered high school—Regina High School, an all-girls Catholic school—and found my "tribe," a fitting description for a Cleveland girl. Each of us had our favorite player or two (pitcher "Sudden Sam" McDowell was mine, although the scrappy center fielder Vic Davalillo was a close second). We followed the games on radio during the week and on television on the weekends. We had our own rituals: on opening day, when most schools allowed students to leave early in order to attend the game, we dressed appropriately to mark the occasion—dresses or skirts and nylons. It was always bitter cold and, I have to be honest, the experience was usually not as fun as it should have been, and the Indians always seemed to lose (actually, they were .500, 1964–1969, per the record books). But, my friends and I knew that there was a right way and a wrong way to mark the beginning of the season, and the right way was to understand its appropriate pageantry and dress to do it honor.

I imagine that this spectator relationship with the game makes it a different kind of game than the one that boys understood. If you actually had the opportunity to play the different positions, then you would have muscle memory. When, at a much later time, in my late twenties in Cincinnati, I played a weekly pickup game with my colleagues in the English Department at the University of Cincinnati, I was always the second baseman. My arm wasn't strong, so putting me in the middle of the field (NOT at shortstop—heavens!) made me less a liability. But a curious and telling feature of my ability was that, even if I could not field the position as well as I wanted to, I *knew*, pretty often, where the ball would be going once it was hit, and was heading in that direction even as the batter swung. I was "reading" the batter: understanding the grammar of the game trumped muscle memory.

It has been more than 50 years since I was pulled into the enchantment of baseball by Sister Judith and Duane Decker. It has been exactly 50 years (plus a few months) since the white-knuckle tension of listening to Sonny Seibert's no-hitter. In the years since, I have experienced heartbreak and misery. As I have told friends, "Being a Cleveland Indians fan builds character." I have lots of character.

As I write this, the Cleveland Indians are heading to the World Series. They will play either the Chicago Cubs (talk about character building!) or the Los Angeles Dodgers. I have my Indians regalia. I am all set. I hope they win. But even if they do not, I will revel in reading each game—anticipating each pitch, scrutinizing the defense, holding my breath between pitches. Experiencing a vivid and continuous dream.

Becoming a Yankees Fan During the Horace Clarke Years

DAVID WOLIN

As every baseball fan knows, New York City was the center of the baseball universe in the 1940s, '50s and '60s. The Yankees' glory days of Yogi, Mickey and Whitey; Duke Snider, Jackie Robinson and the Brooklyn Dodgers; Willy Mays and the Giants; and even the 1969 Miracle Mets. But those days were ancient history to me when I first started following Major League baseball.

My earliest MLB memory was our babysitter trying to watch the 1969 World Series on our family's black and white TV while my brothers and I were running around the house. I have a vague recollection of the Mets playing in the series, but at the time, I had no interest in watching the game.

Six months later, I started following baseball. It was 1970 and I was seven years old. The Dodgers and Giants were long gone from New York. The Yankees last played in the World Series when I was two, and the last player from their glory years, Mickey Mantle, retired before the 1969 season. The Miracle Mets were the defending World Series champions and owned the city.

Most of the other kids in the neighborhood had become Mets fans. It may be that I was born in the Bronx or that I have always been a natural contrarian, but I became a Yankees fan. A Yankees fan in the midst of what would be known as the Horace Clarke Era.

Horace Clarke was the regular second baseman for the Yankees from 1967 to 1974, coming up to the Major League club in 1965 and replacing Bobby Richardson as the Yankees starting second baseman two years later. Clarke was not a bad player, having a career batting average of .256 with 27 home runs, 304 RBIs and 151 stolen bases. His stats are comparable to Bobby Richardson's, who was the Yankee's second baseman during the previous decade, but the Yankees did not make the playoffs once during Clarke's tenure.

Richardson played in seven World Series. Luckily for me, I only had to endure the last five years of the Horace Clarke Era.

I do not know whether to feel sorry for Horace Clarke for having one of the worst stretches of Yankees' history named after him. Otherwise, he would be forgotten in baseball history.

Unfortunately for Horace Clarke, he was not surrounded by the likes of Mickey Mantle, Roger Maris, Tony Kubek and Whitey Ford like Bobby Richardson was. The 1970 Yankees' lineup was not a powerhouse. But even 46 years later, I still remember the names of each of the starting players from that non-descript team surrounding Horace Clarke. Danny Cater, Gene Michael, Jerry Kenney, Roy White, Bobby Mercer, Curt Blefary and a rookie, Thurman Munson, could never be called a Murderer's Row. The starting pitchers Mel Stottlemyre, Fritz Peterson, Stan Bahnsen and Mike Kekich comprised a decent staff but did not come close to the Orioles starters of that era, which included Mike Cuellar, Dave McNally and Jim Palmer. Unfortunately, that mediocre 1970 team may have been the best Yankee's team of the Horace Clarke Era. They won 93 games, but still finished 15 games behind Earl Weaver's great Orioles team.

By 1970, my family and I were living in the New Jersey suburbs, and my father would drive my brothers and me in his Plymouth Valiant to the original Yankees Stadium three or four times a season. My mother never came with us. She was probably happy to have a day without three boys running around the house. But she would make us sandwiches for the game. My father would buy us sodas.

Yankees Stadium was crumbling by 1970 and would be renovated a few years later, but to me it was the greatest place on earth. I only remember sitting behind a column once.

In the early 1970s, I thought the games were a lot shorter than they are today. All the Major League games I attended as a kid were only six innings long because we were already loaded in the Plymouth and on our way home before the seventh inning began so we could beat the traffic on the Major Deegan Expressway and the George Washington Bridge.

Those three or four games we attended each year were all giveaway days at the original Yankees Stadium. Each season, we got Yankees insignia balls, gloves, caps and bats. In those days, they gave away real Louisville Slugger Little League bats, not the miniature bats or the T-shirts they give away these days with MasterCard logos larger than Yankees insignia. However, I do have to admit that some of the new giveaways are an improvement. I would have loved to have had a Ralph Houk bobblehead doll on my dresser.

I had no knowledge of baseball history or even Yankees history when I attended my first bat day. I knew nothing about Babe Ruth, Joe DiMaggio, Lou Gehrig, Whitey Ford or Yogi Berra. My brothers each got bats engraved with the names of then-current Yankee players. I was hoping for a bat with the name of my favorite player, Bobby Murcer. I was handed a bat with the name of a player written in script that I never heard of, M-I-C-K-E-Y (I knew those letters) M-A-N-T-L-E (Who?). I remember practically being in tears over a bat from an unknown player until my father traded the bat to a guy in the row behind us for a precious Bobby Murcer bat. I'm not sure what my father was thinking when I traded the Mickey Mantle bat, but I was happy. Obviously, I would have no future in the sports memorabilia business.

Ironically, Bobby Murcer was supposed to be the next Mickey Mantle. He was another Oklahoma native who came up through the Yankees Minor Leagues system as a power-hitting shortstop. He eventually succeeded Mantle as the Yankees center fielder in 1969. Murcer was a four-time All-Star with the Yankees, having his best seasons from 1970 to 1974, which were my first four seasons as a Yankees fan. He had a Mantle-like day in 1970 when he hit four consecutive home runs in a doubleheader against the Cleveland Indians, but he never put up Mantle-like numbers for his career. However, I revered him in the same way the previous generation revered Mantle.

Like many kids, I went to bed each night with the Yankees game playing on my nightstand clock radio, listening to Frank Messer, Bill White and Phil Rizzuto. They were the Yankees radio and TV broadcasters during most of that era. They would rotate their announcing duties, two of them on TV and one on radio for a three-inning stretch. Those were the days before Rizzuto would leave the stadium in the sixth inning to avoid traffic on the bridge. Clearly, avoiding bridge traffic was a thing back then.

Frank Messer was a traditional baseball announcer, but Phil Rizzuto, together with Bill White, were perfect broadcasters for the Horace Clarke years. Rizzuto spent almost as much time talking about his wife Cora, his son Scooter and daughter-in-law Ann, than he did the game. Hardly a game would go by without him wishing a Happy Birthday to Aunt Minnie or some other relative or friend. Fans loved his famous "Holy Cow" line, but listeners were not always sure what happened on the play. "Holy Cow, you got to see that play" was not too enlightening when you are in bed listening to the game on the radio. But eventually he would get the listeners caught up on the game. Rizzuto made the Yankees a lot more fun to listen to during those years. But after growing up listening to Rizzuto's antics, it made it tough to listen to other teams' announcers. When traveling to cities like Boston or Baltimore, it was difficult to listen to announcers who actually focused on the game

For a Jewish kid growing up in New Jersey, the emergence of Ron Blomberg may have been the most exciting thing to happen in the 1971 season. Although Blomberg came up with the Yankees in 1969, he was injured in 1970 and did not play that year. Blomberg was the only Jewish player that my friends from Hebrew School and I were aware of and he immediately became a hero to us. Once again, my extensive baseball knowledge back then did not include players like Hank Greenberg or Sandy Koufax. Later, in Hebrew School, we learned about Koufax choosing to observe Yom Kippur over pitching in the World Series. Luckily for Ron Blomberg, he would not have to face that same dilemma during the Horace Clarke Era.

The scene at the old Yankees Stadium in those days could not be compared to the excitement at the renovated stadium during the Reggie Jackson years or the Derek Jeter years or even the grandeur of the new palace the Yankees now play in across the street from the old stadium. I remember a July night in 1972, when my friend's father took my friend, his younger brother, and me to a game against the Cleveland Indians. We had great seats, only a few rows behind home plate, in what would be the equivalent of the Legends luxury seats today. For better or worse, there were no investment bankers, celebrities or anyone else on expense accounts in the box seats that evening. Although it was a beautiful evening for baseball in the Bronx, we were surrounded by a sea of empty seats. The Yankees averaged around 15,000 fans a game that year, but I would be surprised if there were more than a few thousand in attendance that night. The stadium was so quiet that night that Ron Blomberg could hear his biggest fans cheering for him. We were thrilled when he turned at home plate to acknowledge us. He may have just wanted us to shut up, but we were thrilled just the same. There was no need to leave early that night to avoid traffic.

The early 1970s Yankees were also the subjects of our Rabbi's sermon one Friday night in 1973, but it had nothing to do with baseball or even Ron Blomberg. The sermon was about two pitchers in the Yankees' starting rotation, Fritz Peterson and Mike Kekich, who swapped wives and even families. At age 10, the scandal did not register much with me, nor did I listen closely enough to know the moral of the sermon, but I thought it was cool that the Rabbi spoke about the Yankees. Luckily for Peterson and Kekich, Rupert Murdoch did not buy the New York Post until 1976. The issue blew over relatively quickly and both players remained on the team for the season.

Even though the Yankees did not make the playoffs during the first half of the 1970s, I became a bigger Yankees fan and true baseball fan in general. I would watch or listen on the radio to the league championship series and World Series with the Orioles, Pirates and the Big Red Machine, even though the Yankees were usually out of the race by early September. I even endured the cross-town Mets winning the National League Pennant in 1973, with former Yankee Yogi Berra as manager. Since I never knew what it was like for the Yankees to win it all, I could live with them coming in second or third.

It was not until 1975, that I suffered real disappointment as a Yankees fan when they traded Bobby Murcer to the San Francisco Giants for Bobby

Bonds. I cursed General Manager Gabe Paul for trading away my hero. I still had the Bobby Murcer bat.

Even though the Yankees sold Horace Clarke to the San Diego Padres in 1974, the Horace Clarke Era did not really end until Chris Chambliss hit the walk-off league championship series-winning home run against the Royals, giving the Yankees the American League Pennant in 1976. Watching that game after school on our family's 24-inch Panasonic color TV, I never jumped so high in my life.

In the years following the Horace Clarke Era, I became another insufferable Yankees fan, expecting the team to win every year. Maybe it is pure nostalgia or the innocence of a seven-year-old following his team, but I now look back and appreciate becoming a fan of the team before it became The Bronx Zoo, before George Steinbrenner and before the Yankees became the Evil Empire to the rest of the league. I would not trade the Pennants and World Championships to come, but in those years, the Yankees were just another team in the league. Until the team was sold to the Steinbrenner family, CBS was no freer with the corporate checkbook than Calvin Griffith in Minnesota or Tom Yawkey in Boston. It was not a team of free agents, mercenaries and media hounds.

It was also the time before the Yankees played for tabloid headlines. George Steinbrenner knew that headlines on the back page of the *New York Post* and *The Daily News* sold tickets. It was before Reggie and Billy, before drug testing and steroid suspensions. Following the Yankees in the early 1970s really was a time of innocence for the Yankees and for me.

After the Yankees won the World Series in 1977, I forgave Gabe Paul for trading Bobby Murcer.

But now I wish I could get that Mickey Mantle bat back.

Get a Shower Before Someone Gets Hurt

Julie E. Townsend

Sometimes, greatness comes in humble people-packages, like Martin B. Little. Does the "B" stand for bodacious, body-builder, or for his love of baseball? At the age of nine, Martin played the outfield for a Little League team in West Jefferson, North Carolina, on a field surrounded by the Appalachian Mountains. Then he had an epiphany. "It's still so vivid, I was walking in from the outfield and as I came across the infield a baseball was lying on the pitcher's mound. Our catcher was at home plate, so I picked up the baseball and motioned for him to squat behind home plate. I wound up and threw what was pretty much a perfect strike. And at that moment I knew that baseball was *my thing*."

He wanted to be a professional pitcher. He says he doesn't know why or how that came into his mind, but he would set his hopes on this dream. "Baseball was something I was good at," he says. But Martin isn't bragging. He happens to be quite self-deprecating, so he finishes the baseball comment with a self-dig. For those who know him, this is his modus operandi.

Many people dream the big dream, on a whisper, a self-repeating mantra. Many don't dare to let others know of their dreams for fear of jinxing themselves. Martin, however, made it his spoken-out-loud dream.

By the time Martin was a senior in high school in 1977, he was recruited by the Philadelphia Phillies. No wonder the Phillies wanted him. He struck out 17 players in a row, in one game alone. That was after he played a 15-inning game, striking out 31 players. Wes Livengood, a major league scout, arranged a meeting with the Phillies, but Martin says he got spooked and didn't sign with them. He was their number 15 draft pick. He calls himself a "fool" for not signing then.

Martin says he hadn't told anyone he'd decided not to sign. "I decided

I just wanted to get married and get a job and not see my dream come true." Livengood came to his house on a Sunday afternoon and Martin announced to everyone that he'd decided not to sign. "My parents thought I had lost my mind. I was just this kid from the mountains of North Carolina. I didn't know what to do."

After a year of working on the housekeeping staff of the local hospital, cleaning 20–30 bathrooms a day along with mopping and scrubbing, Martin decided maybe baseball was a good idea after all. He called Coach Bill Jarrett who had taken an early interest in him.

Coach Jarrett was from next-door Alleghany County in North Carolina, and he found Martin a tryout camp for the St. Louis Cardinals in Gastonia, North Carolina. He even drove Martin down there. Martin had enormous respect for Jarrett, and was well acquainted with the coach—his teams were rivals to Martin's high school. Despite the rivalry, Coach Jarrett saw Martin's raw talent and believed in his abilities. Trying out with fifty other players, Martin was the 14th draft pick for the St. Louis Cardinals.

When they asked him what he wanted for a signing bonus, Martin says, "I really didn't know what to say, so Coach Jarrett said I'd take the same as what the Phillies had offered the year before." It was a $5,000 signing bonus. Martin said, "Of course I would have signed for nothing, just to get the chance to play." His starting salary was $500 a month.

In his first year, he played in the Appalachian Rookie League. He and his wife moved to Johnson City, Tennessee. "I was at the bottom of the totem pole," he says. "Most of the players were right out of high school. We had to work our way up." At first, he was a relief pitcher. In Johnson City, he faced off with Cal Ripken, Jr. Cal, he says, hit a home run off one of Martin's 90 mph pitches. His average was 88 mph at the time.

"It was like being in the movie, *Bull Durham*. The pay wasn't much, but we were all living our dream." He continues, "That movie was the closest to what playing minor league baseball was like. We had our flakes, intellectuals, and everything in between." He laughs as he began to recall Dennis Gadowsky. "Dennis was from Cleveland, and he was so homesick he had to go see his family and girlfriend, but we only had two days off. Dennis was scheduled to pitch a Tuesday night game against the Elizabeth Twins. He made it back in time, but for some reason he had packed his gums with chewing tobacco. He didn't know what to do, so he asked one of the boys and they told him to swallow it." Martin laughs again. "I'd never seen anyone look green before. Not only was he tired from his trip, he'd swallowed the chew. He gave up seven runs."

Martin also played with a pitcher named Tony Jordan. "We all called him 'Mad Dog.' He could throw the ball at 100 mph, but he couldn't control it. He had a million dollar arm but 10 cent control." It reminded Martin of the movie *Major League* in which Charlie Sheen played a pitcher whose pitches were out of control. "He'd pack chewing tobacco in both jaws and in his lower lip, all at the same time. He was this white guy with an Afro!" The last time Martin saw Mad Dog pitch he walked 14 batters.

In 1979, Martin went to spring training in Gastonia, North Carolina. He had his sights on playing in the Florida State League in St. Petersburg. The "powers that be," gave him a choice: he could come back to Gastonia as a long reliever and work his way up or go as a starting pitcher to Wisconsin.

Martin went to Wisconsin, where he played with a co-op team, comprised of players from several Minor League teams, including those affiliated with the Seattle Mariners, New York Yankees, and St. Louis Cardinals. During one spring training outing, Martin was excited to have batting practice with the major leaguers. The players and the pitchers lined-up, and he found himself pitching to Ted Simmons, "one of the all-time great Cardinals," Martin says.

If you ask Martin about the worst game he's ever pitched, he'll always tell you about that game against the Phils in Spartanburg, South Carolina. It was a hot Sunday afternoon. Martin says, "I was not having a good game, to say the least. They were hitting rockets." Manager Johnny Lewis went out to the mound to ask the standard question: "How are you feeling?" Martin says, "You always say you're fine. Always. Of course the manager is just killing time until a relief pitcher is warmed up and ready to come in." This day, Lewis replied, "Well, why don't you go on in and get a shower before somebody gets hurt." Of course it wasn't funny at the time, but Martin says "I have to laugh about it now."

Martin's career continued, bouncing from Wisconsin and eventually down to Florida. He was making steady progress, but then he suffered an injury—even though the team doctor said that as far as strength testing went, Martin had, "one of the strongest arms around." If that injury occurred today, *maybe* he would have been fine. But in the early '80s, enormous pain persisted with Martin's pitching, and the trainers and doctors could only speculate on the cause. They didn't know if it was a bone spur or a detached ligament. The surgery would have been risky, lots of rehab would have been required, and there were no assurances he'd regain his pitching velocity and accuracy.

After much frustration and continued pain, Martin returned to the mountains of North Carolina and opened up Ashe County's first gym. The gym still thrives, and through this pathway, Martin has touched and influenced too many lives to count. He still loves baseball. How couldn't he, when he met Hank Aaron and Bob Feller, and played with the likes of Jim Presley, Kent Harbeck, and Gary Gaetti? In fact, Martin recalls that his most memorable game was striking out Harbeck and Gaetti, in a 9 to 4 game. His favorite player was Jim "Catfish" Hunter from North Carolina. "I liked to watch him pitch. Liked his style and form."

Martin still loves the game, watching a pitcher on the mound, scuffing tufts of dust into the air, the shuffling and positioning, the labeled shoes, the smell of the stitched ball and the slapping sound as it pops into the weathered glove. He watches the signs from the catcher, feels the heaviness of the fans anticipation. Martin's crystal blue eyes zero in on the plate … what else would anyone want than to throw another dream pitch? He was able to fulfill his fantasy, short-lived as it may have been. How many of us would dare dream so?

Walk-Off in St. Louis

CAROLINE KANE KENNA

The flags of 11 World Series championships rim Busch Stadium like banners around a castle keep. Inside venders roam the concrete stairs chanting, *"Hot dogs! Peanuts! Cold water! Ice cold beer!"* Popcorn oils the evening air and the scent of sausage, peppers, and onions hangs as heavy as the St. Louis humidity.

Our Cardinals are facing the Los Angeles Dodgers in a three-game home stand in late July that fit into three schedules and satisfied Logan's desire to see St. Louis play. The last time we all saw the Redbirds live, Logan was three years old. This time we had hoped for an aces' battle, pitchers Adam Wainwright or Carlos Martinez against LA's Clayton Kershaw, but Kershaw's on the disabled list and Wainwright and Martinez were winners earlier in a four-game sweep of the San Diego Padres, so those matchups aren't likely.

As we line up and wait for the gates to open, we hear Michael Wacha announced as the starting pitcher. Logan approves. "He has some really filthy stuff," he says, sure the Cards will serve up a series we won't soon forget. Two hours before Friday's first pitch, we flow with the crowd into the stadium, claim Matt Holliday bobble heads—given away with each ticket that day—and soak in the ambiance of being there.

The escalator going up fills with the faithful in red hats, names of current heroes, Molina and Wainwright, Carpenter and Holliday on their backs. There's a buzz of talk about stats, players' names are tossed about, and the expectation that St. Louis has found their groove is discussed.

Logan hopes to snag a ball while Mike and I indulge in the food of real fans—hot dogs and beer that always taste better at the ballpark. We marvel at the cityscape and the Gateway Arch. Look down at home plate and wonder if there's a bad seat in this place. Crowds of over 40,000 not unusual for weekend games in a stadium that is high on baseball fans' lists of places to go.

Mike and I send we-are-here pictures of the field and the St Louis skyline to our older boys. Patrick and Mark may not forgive us anytime soon for choosing this trip when they are busy. A first at this ballpark that has been home to the Cards since 2006, perhaps gives Logan some bragging rights when his older brothers talk about how they ran the bases after a game.

Underneath the upper deck escaping the late afternoon sun, we spy our long-limbed 19-year-old across the field. He glistens in his white jersey and blue Cardinals cap near the visitors' bullpen. He's there with other fans hoping he hasn't missed Cardinals' batting practice. Instead Logan connects "eye-to-eye," with Dodgers' Scott Kazmir. Later Logan displays his prize, and reports the visiting pitcher "smiled and tossed me this ball."

It's the top of the 16th inning; we've been molded to our seats for more hours than I care to count. My husband and I are long past wilted and Logan has his glove on his head instead of his cap. LA's man on second base is the first movement on either side since Jedd Gyorko cracked a Cardinals' home run at the end of the ninth to extend the play.

I'm texting with Mark, who is listening to the game at his home in North Carolina. He says it's time for bed but I reply we're on a mission, not leaving till there's a winner.

History in the making, the longest game the Cards have played all season. In the rivalry between these teams this five hour and 10 minute marathon is number three. St. Louis relief pitcher Seth Maness retires the side and a Midwestern storm begins to brew.

First baseman, Matt Adams, is announced as the Cardinals' pinch hitter. In the wee hours of Saturday, long after the city allows fireworks and the last beer has been sold, anxious electricity charges the faithful. Cheers build and roll like thunder around the stadium as "Big City" Adams steps to the plate. We're all on our feet when the slugger's second swing caps the Cardinals' night.

A solo homer! Cardinal magic on full display. Adams skips and flips his bat and trots around the bases. The dugout empties, teammates celebrating like Little Leaguers. Big City's walk-off, a bookend to Gyorko's comeback fireworks, keeps the winning streak alive.

"One down two to go," Logan said. Hope swirled around us as we high-five our way out of the stadium and past the statue of Stan Musial. Could this be St. Louis's year to win another World Series crown? The last was in 2011, a seven game classic with the Rangers, Tony La Russa the skipper for the Redbirds' run from wildcard to winner.

Who knew our family would fall so hard for the boys of summer? Arriving in the mid–'90s about the same time the Cards hired La Russa, we were East Coasters in a perfect storm of proximity, interest and age. The boys and Mike discovered Little League, how to get out of a pickle and properly swing the bat, as the Cardinals across the Mississippi River returned to their winning ways.

Before long we were a part of the white and red nation singing, "Hey Tony La Russa" to the tune of "The Macarena." We followed the Cards on TV, in the stadium at home and planned trips to ballparks within driving distance. When my brother Tom came to town, a Cardinals game or three, was a part of the plan.

Patrick and Mark studied their favorite players, memorizing batting stances and rituals—some they tried when they played. The boys camped out near the Cards dugout during batting practice hoping to get an autograph or two. Once they came close to taking home a pair of batting gloves that belonged to Edgar Renteria.

Patrick was standing in a knot of young signature hunters with balls and programs, Mark was staked out nearby, when the future Hall of Famer finished pre-game warm ups. Renteria pulled off the gloves and laid them on the roof of the dugout. I guess the shortstop expected one or two of the clamoring kids to pick up the souvenir. Instead, two large adults pushed through the crowd and snatched the gloves from under their noses.

The chance that got away makes a good story when talk turns to Cardinals greats like back flipping Golden Glover Ozzie "Wizard of Oz" Smith, and Willie McGee. When number 25, Mark McGwire, stepped to the plate, the stadium rocked. Flashbulbs popped from the nosebleed section to the seats closest to the field when the king swung his bat.

In 1998, McGwire won the National League hitting title. All eyes were on that who-would-get-there-first rivalry between Sammy Sosa, right fielder for the Chicago Cubs, and Big Mac, the Cardinal first baseman. The single season back and forth shattered home run records, first Babe Ruth's 60 then Roger Maris's 61. Sosa slammed 66 but the redhead with Popeye arms belted 70.

We were at Busch Memorial in August when Big Mac moved closer to the home run crown. He rocketed one into twilight against the Atlanta Braves. The boys were ready with their gloves if that piece of history had landed in the upper deck. A month later, we gathered around the TV. The Cards faced the Cubs. McGwire tied Maris's record on September 7, and broke it the following day.

That was before there was an asterisk in the record book for performance enhancing drugs. Some say the slugfest was a sham because both were users but for us, that summer memory still shines.

McGwire, formerly of the Oakland Athletics, joined the Cardinals in 1997. Logan was born that year. At six weeks old, dressed in a Cardinals' onesie he slept in his stroller at the stadium's Homer's Landing. While his brothers sweated every pitch as if they were Cardinal batters and fielders,

Logan toddled between Mike and me. His head protected by a red plastic batters' helmet, he'd crow, "Mark McGwire" and slap hands until he fell asleep against my shoulder.

In the new stadium on a Saturday more than 15 years later, Logan worries the leather on his glove. Adams homers again but the Redbirds fail to fly. The rest of that sultry weekend, the Cardinal bats are quiet and their gloves are sloppy. Boilerplate 101 plays Logan learned as a Little Leaguer in Indiana are blown.

The longer-than-normal game shakes up the roster. Players reserved for later in the series start game two while regulars, like catcher Yadier Molina, rest. LA batters pound pitcher Mike Leake. On Sunday evening, the Cards elevate Mike Mayers from Triple A Memphis to pitch in place of Tyler Lyons. Great as a reliever on Friday night, Lyons isn't ready to take the mound. Mayers gives up a grand slam in his 1⅓ inning debut and gets no back up from his defense. That "welcome to the Major Leagues" reminds me of a Little League game Patrick played in. No matter what the pitcher tried, he couldn't find the plate and kept walking runs home.

By the seventh inning stretch the crowd in the stadium thins to mostly LA fans. Kazmir, the pitcher who threw Logan the ball, wins his Sunday match up. The series' two wins, one loss build momentum for the Dodgers' season that perhaps carries into the play-offs.

For the Cardinals, that home stand is fraught like the rest of 2016 season. In the end St. Louis falls one game short of the post-season berth for the first time in five years. The last time that happened was in 2010, the following year the Cards won the World Series. We'll probably dissect the season over turkey this Thanksgiving. But soon questions about Mike Matheny's managing style will give way to concerns about how much longer Molina may play and who might replace Holliday as a leader in the clubhouse.

Our affinity for St. Louis is one of the threads that holds our family together. It has outlasted McGwire and his 70 home runs; Albert Pujols, hero of the World Series in 2006 against the Detroit Tigers; and La Russa's retirement. We mourned with the nation in 2002, when in the middle of the season pitcher Darrell Kile suddenly died. We were stunned silent when rising star Oscar Taveras was killed in a car crash 10 days after the 2014 season ended.

We carried our love for the red-and-white to Indiana where the Chicago Cubs are the home team and to North Carolina, baseball no man's land between the Washington Nationals and the Atlanta Braves. Even now Patrick proudly wears his Cardinals' colors in Philadelphia, and when Mark was in Singapore last year he found a way to keep up with his team.

But the five of us are Johnny-come-lately fans for the franchise on the banks of the Mississippi River. Always a part of the National League, the team was officially named the Cardinals around 1900, when a newspaper nickname was adopted. The Missouri club boasts 19 National League pennants and 13 division crowns and 28 post-season appearances in those years. Countless legends of the game like "Dizzy" Dean, Stan "the Man" Musial, Enos Slaughter and Red Schoendienst have worn the Cardinals uniform. Pitcher Bob Gibson fanned 3,117 batters in his 17 years in front of some of the best fans in the Major Leagues.

We have cheered the Cards since 1995 and in that time there have been some amazing comebacks, none more exciting than game six of the 2011 World Series. The Redbirds, on the brink of elimination, came back to St. Louis to win it all.

In North Carolina, Logan and I yelled at the TV through 11 innings as if we were in the stadium. For a while Mark, at Appalachian State, and I were texting. Later, Patrick called from Atlanta. He had taken a study break and gotten caught up in the seesaw, holding his breath as the Cardinals, twice down to their final strike, just kept fighting back. David Freese, MVP and St. Louis native, drove in the winning run, a feat that earns him a standing ovation each time he comes to the plate, even when he went on to play for a division foe, the Pittsburgh Pirates.

That's the thing about baseball: It is an optimists' sport. With each batter comes an opportunity to be a hero the fans remember. One catch can fire up a team or change the course of any given game. A stolen base could tilt the scale.

Around the first of the year, the boys start counting the days till spring training, talking about who has been added to the Cardinals' roster, how our Redbirds will reclaim the top spot in the Central Division.

Who's the next breakout player? Will Lance Lynn be back on the mound? They'll wonder if Waino will be a beast, if Carlos will continue to shine and, if Trevor Rosenthal becomes a starter, will Jaime Garcia move to the bullpen?

What about the bats of Adams, Gyorko and Aledmys Diaz? Will Matt Carpenter stay the leadoff hitter? If Stephen Piscotty and Randall Grichuk improve their defense in the off-season, will it be enough to keep the Cubs and the Pirates at bay?

We'll agree that St. Louis wins World Series titles in uneven years, and perhaps the 2017 Cards will capture the 12th pennant for the rim of Busch Stadium.

Love, Hate, Cubs

David E. Malehorn

To my new grandson Booker:

I hope that you fall in love with something good while you are still a very young boy. By the time I was four, I was already a Cubs fan. This has not always been a good thing, but love doesn't always make you happy.

I was born in 1962 BC. BC stands for *before cable*. I grew up on the west edge of Chicagoland, where we could use something called an *antenna*, on something called a *black-and-white* TV, to get a pretty good picture on Channel 9, WGN. Also in 1962, the National League decided to play 162 games instead of 154, maybe just so the Cubs could lose more. The Cubs liked losing 103 times so much in 1962, that they lost 103 times again in 1966.

By then I was watching a lot of those losses on TV. My Mom and Dad were teachers, so my Grandma took care of me in the afternoons, after morning preschool. Grandma would feed me an egg salad sandwich for lunch and then send me to the back bedroom, where I turned on the TV for naptime. The first pitch was at 1:30 p.m., because Wrigley Field did not yet have something called *lights*.

On TV, Mr. Jack Brickhouse would call the games as best he could, like your nice uncle trying to say something good about your bad school play. Sometimes he would shout, "Back, back, back—Hey, Hey!" which would wake me, but mostly these were quiet, soothing games. They pointed the TV cameras at more pleasant things, like women's' hats, or sailboats out on Lake Michigan.

In 1967, things started to change. It was nice to hear Mr. Brickhouse sound happy, and it was more fun to stay awake and watch the Cubs. My Dad told me, "All you really want is a better-than-even chance of seeing them win." This doesn't seem like much to ask for, but the Cubs had had a winning season only one time since he was in high school.

The Cubs pitcher, Mr. Ferguson Jenkins, was so good in 1967 that he almost won a prize called the *Cy Young*. The size of the crowds at Wrigley went up by more than half, and the team finished with a winning record, something it would do for five more years! Fergie stayed good, and he finally got that Cy Young Award in 1971.

Other Cubs players were good too, and I still remember their names: Holtzman, Hundley, Banks, Beckert, Santo, Kessinger, Hickman, Williams. Several of them were among the best players ever, and we honor them in a baseball museum called the *Hall of Fame*.

Sometimes an old man would come out of the dugout and kick dirt, or yell about things. He wasn't a player then, he was something called a *manager*. His name was Mr. Leo Durocher, and he is in the Hall of Fame too, but not for dirt kicking or yelling. I think it's because he got his players to try harder, and it helped them win more games.

Booker, it's still hard for me to talk about 1969. It started great, but ended badly. Grown-ups told me things to try and make me understand. They said, "What goes up, must come down." Sometimes that is a good thing. That summer, astronauts went up to the moon, and we all watched them on TV to make sure that they came back down safely.

The Cubs flew pretty high too. They were in first place for April, May, June, July and August. People were over the moon about it. Mr. Santo starting hopping up and clicking his heels after wins. On TV and radio they played a song called, "Hey, Hey, Holy Mackerel." I can still sing that song, Booker.

After Labor Day I went back to being a school kid, going into second grade with Mrs. Venturoni. She was pretty, and she let me take math with the third-graders. After Labor Day, the Cubs went back to being the Cubs, going into a slump when they lost eight straight games. It wasn't pretty, and that was when the Mets passed them in the standings and never looked back.

Grown-ups had told me, "Don't count your chickens before they're hatched," but it was too late. I had counted on them to win it all, but the Cubs laid a big egg in September. Between Labor Day and my birthday two weeks later, they went from five games up to four games back. Now when the "Hey, Hey" song came on, I sang along, angrily. When they got to, "The Cubs are on their way," I chimed in, "to last place!" I was seven years old, and I was already bitter.

By watching the Cubs as a young kid during the 1960s, I cut my teeth on the taste of disappointment. This affected my next 50 years of trying to be a fan. Booker, maybe you should love something more dependable, like reading, or stamps. If you do fall for baseball, though, there's some stuff you need to know if you're going to grow up with your heart still in one piece.

It can be hard to stay in love.

In 1970 my Dad changed jobs, and I had to finish growing up in a different town. On moving day our parents drove us south on the interstate highway. We left the city behind, we left the suburbs behind, and then we were out in the countryside. There was a lot of it. We drove for hours.

"That's corn, and those are soybeans," Mom told us. She looked out the window at the horizon for a while. "Pretend it's an ocean—the grain elevators are like ships!" Finally the road went down and up a big hill as we came to the city limits of Charleston. "See how the land gets hilly here?" Mom asked. "This is a terminal moraine!" She wanted us to know that this little town was more important than it looked. Glaciers ground to a halt here and unloaded. So did we.

In a few weeks it was Labor Day and time to go back to school. In the mornings I waited down the block for the school bus. There were tough-looking older kids wearing ball caps with words like PIONEER and TREFLAN. They fought over who made better tractors. Some days I would crawl under a bush, cover myself with dead leaves, and hide.

It didn't impress my classmates that I was from Chicago, or a Cubs fan. Most of them rooted for the Cardinals. I didn't understand–I thought everyone should root for the Cubs. It was the loyal thing to do in Illinois, like rooting for Abe Lincoln.

It turned out Illinois was made up of different parts where people liked different things. Chicago and St. Louis were like two big magnets pulling Cubs fans in one direction, and Cardinals fans in the other. It was hard for me to live in-between.

I was still drawn to the Cubs but Chicago was far, far away. We couldn't get channel 9 on TV, even with a rotating antenna on a tall pole on top of the house. Some nights I could get Cubs games on the radio, twisting the tuning knob as the signal faded in and out of the static. I was deep in enemy territory and losing touch with home base.

I was closer to St. Louis now, but only physically. The Cardinals repelled me. They played in dingy downtown St Louis in a concrete coliseum with obnoxious red seats and phony plastic grass. Inside Busch Stadium was a sweltering pit where suffering players put wet towels on their heads, and pitiful Clydesdales pulled a beer wagon around. This wasn't baseball—it was a hellish marketing scheme to sell Budweiser.

And yet my cocky classmates liked those infernal Redbirds. Maybe this was because since their kindergarten days, they had watched the Cardinals go to two World Series, and win one. All I had to show since kindergarten was 1969.

And that wasn't the Cubs' only collapse. Five more times during the 1970s they would be in first place for a while early on, only to take a mid-summer nosedive. My Dad said people were calling it the *June swoon*. It was hard for me to defend a team so good at being bad that there was a new word for it.

Your love might not repay your affection.

I was a pretty smart kid, Booker, and I began to see another pattern too. Every time a player got good, he got gone. The Wrigley family didn't want to pay them what they were worth, and ditched them like used chewing gum.

A brash, young Cubs player named Bill Madlock won the batting title, but by the time I could brag on him, my classmates were proudly sporting T-shirts that said, "118 Club," for Lou Brock's gaudy stolen base record. It hurt when I learned that Brock had once played for the Cubs, but they had stupidly traded him away—to the Cardinals.

It seemed there were an awful lot of great players who had once played for the Cubs. Soon enough the Cubs traded Bill Madlock away too, right after he won another batting title. A couple years later, Cubs reliever Bruce Sutter saved 37 games and won the Cy Young. Naturally, the following year the Cubs traded him, too—to the Cardinals!

My loyalty was sorely tested. The hurt started to feel like hate. I referred to my own team as a *major league farm club*. I started yelling, "Former Cub!" whenever it applied, while watching other teams' highlights on the TV news.

Love deserves second chances.

When I was finishing high school, my home changed into a kind of boarding house. I was the last of four kids, so my parents started renting out the empty bedrooms to college students. Maybe to ease the transition, we had cable TV installed.

I was thrilled to find that we got WGN again, and I happily reconnected with my suburban Chicago childhood. I watched vintage cartoons on Ray Rayner's kiddie show before school. In the afternoons I did homework in front of old Mickey Mouse Club reruns.

I could watch the Cubs now too, so I decided to give them another chance. Jack Brickhouse was still calling the games the best he could, like your philosophical uncle trying to say something constructive about your poor life choices. In 1980 he really got a workout, sugarcoating 16 different losing streaks of three or more games.

Booker, I know they say, "It's not whether you win or lose, it's how you play the game," but how the Cubs played was *bad*. That year they led the league in errors and striking out, and in giving up walks and runs. They fit right in with WGN's lineup of Looney Tunes, but it wasn't very funny to me.

Love can mess with your head.

This felt more like a bad flashback. Every time I turned on the TV and tuned in a game, the Cubs dropped out of contention. Like victims do, I blamed myself. I began to think I was jinxing the team just by watching them on TV. I started changing the channel after the early innings to give the Cubs a better chance of winning.

Pretty soon my girlfriend found out about my preoccupation with the Cubs. We watched the games together, and I explained the basics of baseball to her, aided by the abundant evidence onscreen of how not to do things. She saw my frustration and she shared my pain.

This was no act. It turns out she was a real convert, and not just to the sport, but to the Cubs, heartache and all. I count this as one of the great achievements of my life. Teaching my girlfriend to love the Cubs was a successful way to wind up married to a woman who was used to disappointment.

That girlfriend is your Grandma Lois. You should be so lucky someday, Booker.

You have to have it happen to you, to know how it feels.

Just as Lois was climbing aboard the Cubs' broken-down bandwagon, the Wrigley's sold the ball club. This changes everything, I thought. Surely the Tribune Company would put a better team on the field—winning sells more papers and gets better TV ratings.

On WGN, the new face of the Cubs was Harry Caray, a white-haired, loose-lipped, good-time Charlie peering out through huge glasses with lenses as thick as beer mugs. Harry called games as he saw them, like your tipsy uncle, unafraid to say something outrageous about your boring wedding reception. Harry made every fan feel like a Bleacher Bum. He was a huge hit.

On the field, the new Cubs at first looked like a rerun, floundering to fifth place in 1982 and 1983. But there were some glimmers. All-Star Leon Durham—consolation prize from the Cardinals in the Sutter trade—led a resurgence in hitting, and the Cubs led the league in slugging in 1983.

The Cubs pitchers had the league's highest ERA those years too. That's a bad thing, Booker. Fergie Jenkins came back after a decade away, but he was wearing out, and after 1983 he retired. Reliever Lee Smith was a bright spot in the bullpen, and he got his first trip to the All Star Game.

Then there was this new kid Ryne Sandberg. He was a real good looker, according to Lois. As soon as the Cubs moved him to second base, he won a Gold Glove, his first of nine in a row.

The signs were still good when 1984—that fabled, ominous year—finally rolled around. Lois and I graduated from college and got married in May. That month, the Cubs took sole possession of first place for the first time in nearly six years.

In June, Lois and I set up household, and I started graduate school. I charted the Cubs' wins and losses on a long piece of graph paper on the wall of my office. That line started to sag a bit, but two things happened to ward off another June swoon.

First, the Cubs traded for a redheaded giant from Cleveland. Pitcher

Rick Sutcliffe put the team on his big back, and he would go 16–1 on his way to the Cy Young award. You couldn't wait to see his next start—it was like watching a Disney movie, Booker, it was so magical.

The same week Sutcliffe arrived, Ryne Sandberg—who was on his way to the MVP—had his own movie moment. On national TV in a win against the Cardinals, Sandberg tied it twice with homers in the bottom of the 9th, and in the bottom of the 10th. Both blasts were off of Bruce Sutter, the former Cub!

All summer I tracked the Cubs' rise on my wall chart at work. By the first of August, they had put the Mets behind them and were in first place to stay. When the Cubs clinched the division in September, I was more than happy to put the memory of 1969 behind me.

But I was nervous, Booker. Playoffs were unknown territory for me. What goes up higher must come down harder, I figured.

The league championship series against the Padres started with two midweek day games at Wrigley, which still had no lights. I brought a little TV to my office, and grimly closed the door. When the first game quickly turned into a rout, then I opened the door and shared the good news. Sutcliffe himself had homered; this seemed like destiny.

After the second game and second Cubs win, I had to admit the pennant was a lock. The Cubs only needed to win one of three games out west. Learning nothing from 1969, I counted this San Diego chicken way before it could ever hatch.

The Cubs got a sound beating in Game 3. My faith started to crack. There were still two chances left to win one game, but this now felt like long odds.

That weekend, my parents came to visit, and they took Lois and me out for dinner. Game 4 was on a TV over the bar, too far away to hear over the Saturday night crowd in the restaurant. But from the cheers and groans and yelling in the bar we could tell when the Cubs took the lead, then lost it, then tied it up again.

I fidgeted and struggled to stay in the conversation with my parents and my new wife, trying hard not to look past them at the flickering picture on a faraway screen. I realized that this was a watershed moment for me. Finally the grown-up inside my head told the young boy inside my heart that there are more important things in life than baseball.

That's when Steve Garvey hit a walk-off homer to win it for the Padres.

Technically, there was still Game 5, but it was clear what Fate had already decided, and this was simply confirmed the next day. We watched sadly at home as Sutcliffe stayed in too long, Durham let a grounder go through his legs, Sandberg missed another on a bad hop, and the Cubs blew their lead, the game, and the pennant.

"They wouldn't be the Cubs," I said to Lois.

"If they didn't break your heart," she replied.

We've said it often, in our 32 years together. Misery loves company, like they say.

Tis better to have loved and lost, than never to have loved at all.—Tennyson

As Fate would have it, Booker, you picked a good year to join the family. When you were born in April, the Cubs were already in first place, and they stayed there for the rest of the season. This wasn't unexpected—they were pretty good the year before too.

Then it finally happened. The Cubs won the division series, the pennant, and then the World Series, in an epic Game 7 more improbable than a Disney movie. Fans everywhere jumped, cheered, and gathered in streets, delirious and bit stunned: a century of frustration had just ended with a groundout to third.

The last time the Cubs won it all, there was no Wrigley Field, the flag had 46 stars, and there were only eight planets. A lot of time and people had passed. Now fans lifted glasses and tearfully toasted announcers and players who hadn't lived to see this day. They left Cubs items on the graves of loved ones, and wept for their years of wasted hope.

Newspapers said that the curse had been broken, and bad memories had been erased. I'm not sure I agree. I can still recall the playoff heartbreaks of 1984, 1989, 1998, 2003, 2007, 2008, and 2015. But who's counting?

Those were all winning seasons, with some truly great players. Those years weren't wasted, and they won't be forgotten. Your Grandma Lois and I have decades of shared memories, even from the losing seasons. Ask her about Andre Dawson some time, or Greg Maddux.

The curse was really self-inflicted. People looked backwards through the long lens of history, focusing only on the missing championships. That just magnified the disappointment. It's time to look forward again.

Love never fails.

It takes a blessing to break a curse, Booker, and you're blessed with a fresh start. Until they win it again, you'll be able to say you were born the year the Cubs last won the World Series. I hope this doesn't last so long this time, but repeating isn't easy and it might be a while.

If you focus on the people and the pastime, though, and not just on the playoffs, you'll get something called *perspective*. It helps us see more than just wins and losses in a season. Keep your eye on the ballgame, stay tuned to the present, and listen to the play-by-play. The more you study the thing you love, the more things about it you'll find to love.

Winning is terrific. Celebrate it, but don't always expect it. Losing hurts, but pain is the rent we pay to live here, and it fades. Every new game is a clean score sheet and nine fresh innings of hope. This is something called a *metaphor*, which helps us see more than just baseball in an essay.

Life is really all about the journey you're on and the loved ones you share it with. That never changes. Booker, whether you're headed for an up year or a down year, the playoffs or the cellar, take someone's hand, and remember to stop and smell the ivy along the way.

Mom, Dad, Ernie and Paul

STEPHEN P. WARD

I can count on two hands the times Dad joined me in the back yard to play catch. With fingers left over.

But always a masterful educator, he created one father-son experiential baseball seminar, the highlights of which I can still relive, vividly, after more than 40 years.

The year 1973 was my first as a young fan. On September 22, as the season was winding down, Dad treated me to my first pilgrimage, halfway across our state, to the corner of Michigan and Trumbull in Detroit. Tiger Stadium.

He had done this before with my older brothers, and more frequently when they had lived in Pontiac, a Motor City suburb. Conversation was light in the Delta 88 that Saturday morning. It wasn't that he was withholding some encyclopedic in-car preparation for was about to happen. Dad really wasn't a fan of the game. But he was *my* fan, and his objective was to facilitate—to let me take it all in. This was something major along what he knew would be a spectrum of life experiences.

I had listened to the Tigers regularly that season, but everything that day was new and unexpected. The stadium itself, for starters. I had never thought about what it looked like on the outside. And Tiger Stadium was exceptional. The exterior was entirely white. It gleamed in the low sun of that last day of summer. I had not anticipated anything like the giant light towers that ringed the structure. I wondered why we were next to an expressway and not downtown, as I had imagined. Inside the stadium, I breathed in cigar smoke and spilled beer, both exotic aromas at that point in my young life.

After we worked our way through the crowded concourse and moved to the section number matching our tickets, it happened. The moment that lives inside every baseball lover. That unforgettable first sight of the jewel-green sea of grass, wrapped around the groomed diamond of clay and sand,

73

all surrounded by low, ballpark-green walls and thousands of people in seats that disappeared up into the dark reaches of the massive shrine.

After a few seconds of reverential silence, followed by what felt like floating to our seats, I was swept back into the moment by the voice of public address announcer Joe Gentile, the bouncy chords of the organ, and hawkers' calls for hot dogs and peanuts.

It was at this point that Dad's real mission began. He had briefed me prior to the trip on the use of one of his old cameras, an Exakta Varex. With enough black and white film to get me through the game and the assurance of his guidance, he turned me loose to do what he did when he, a world traveler, was experiencing something for the first time.

We were seated next to the Tigers' bullpen. There, close enough to touch during his pregame warm-up, was *the* Mickey Lolich. I snapped shot after shot. Mickey had a *real* face. That was *truly* an Old English D on his jersey—the same D that, by now, I could draw with my eyes closed.

I have those 8 × 10 photographs to this day. They tell the story of a wide-eyed boy through game-action images with composition framed from turf to upper deck. Everything is there.

And the players: Bill Freehan. Aurelio Rodriguez. Eddie Brinkman. Mickey Stanley. Frank Howard. And Mr. Tiger himself, Al Kaline. Some Red Sox, too. Carl Yastrzemski, Carlton Fisk, Tommy Harper.

Dad's layered lesson continued in the days after that game. He had already visualized the quality time I would spend with my oldest brother, David, 11 years my senior and a budding photojournalist. David had established a darkroom in our basement and, sure enough, I got several hours of lessons in photo processing. I was still mighty young, and I didn't retain the technical details. But the magic of seeing my shots, first as negatives and then as full images slowly appearing on paper in the chemical bath, while working in close quarters with the brother I knew the least, was one of many priceless experiences Dad would orchestrate throughout life.

My treasured album of photos went on to earn a ribbon in the Elliott Elementary School Talent Fair, alongside my first book, *The Joe Smasher Story*, in which I presented the biography of the greatest Tiger to live and play on the field of my imagination. This epic, typed by Mom, was illustrated with my pencil-drawn pictures of Joe and the Tigers in action, inspired by the images I studied in the sports pages of our evening newspaper and often perfected during church sermons.

That I had suddenly, that year, done anything with words was quite an unexpected thrill for Dad and, even more so, Mom. Up to that time, I had given my parents reason to hope and pray that I would be a late bloomer when it came to reading.

When Mom noticed that I had finally brought home a book from the school library, and that it was *The Al Kaline Story*, I think she started to see a real possibility, a palette with which she could work her supreme nurturing skills.

She began to let me sit on the floor in the bookshop of the spacious old Knapp's Department Store in Lansing while she shopped. When it was difficult to get the baseball books out of my hands and back on the shelf, they would come home with us, sometimes with a small sack of sour cherry balls from the Knapp's candy counter. This was the beginning of my library of baseball books that she has continued to stock on birthdays and Christmases through my adult years.

I may have been one of the few 10-year olds with a multi-year subscription to *Baseball Digest* magazine. I pored over my edition of *The Baseball Encyclopedia*, regularly studying the events and names of the past: Cartwright, Spalding, Young, Cobb, and Ruth; DiMaggio, Greenberg, Robinson, and Mays.

Studying baseball built my awareness of the ways in which great thinkers and writers from the 19th century onward have used the game to provide perspective on our national experience. With Mom's help, my bookcase began to welcome works by American historians. Among them was Bruce Catton, who wrote that "Although [baseball] is wholly urbanized it still speaks of the small town in the simple rural era that lived before the automobile came in to blight the landscape. One reason for this is that in a land of unending change, baseball changes very little."

And then there was the radio.

WJR, one of the great full-service stations in American broadcasting, connected our house to Detroit from sunup to sundown. I can still recite the 24-hour program schedule on The Great Voice of the Great Lakes. On summer evenings, my mom worked throughout the house with two men named Ernie and Paul by her side—the Voice of Summer and the Voice of God. Ernie Harwell, the greatest baseball announcer of all time, and Paul Carey, his baritone partner in the booth. It wasn't long before Mom's portable radio made its way to my bedside, and I developed my years-long habit of late-night listening.

Ernie and Paul are forever connected, in my heart and mind, to Mom. Ernie conveyed a gentle soul who had a wealth of stories and told them often. Like Mom. And also like Mom, Paul was kind and humble and showed interest in and respect for everyone. Among his other WJR duties was a high school scoreboard program after the 11 o'clock newscast. He reported every single basketball and football score in the state of Michigan, for 35 years. And he seemed to genuinely know every town and school he named. I always listened attentively to hear him read the name of our town's high school.

Al Kaline reached 3,000 career hits in 1974 during a road game in his hometown of Baltimore, a year and two days after my first game in Detroit. When it was time for the at-bat in which it was likely to happen, Ernie turned over the broadcast play-by-play to Paul, who for most innings handled color commentary. But Ernie Harwell wanted Paul to call it, and Paul did. A double into the right field corner. Perfectly appropriate for the finest right fielder to play the game. Even as a kid, hearing Paul follow the Kaline hit and the ensuing break in the game to celebrate, with a sincere on-air word of thanks to Ernie for allowing him the chance to call baseball history, gave me the lasting highlight of that night. Another lesson in humility, gratitude, and sharing.

To be a fan of Detroit sports teams is to be, at the very least, patient. My boyhood years saw some of the worst seasons ever for the Tigers. I never quite caught on to the weight of this as those years unfolded, though, thanks to Ernie and Paul, who were always positive and civil and always finding ways to make the games interesting and exciting. My faith teaches me to believe in hope. The thrill of hope. And the Tigers have provided years of lessons in hope. As an adult, I credit Mom for my ability to persevere, and I can trace the inspiration and clear influence of Ernie and Paul every time I think that next year will be better.

My parents knew how to foster lifelong interests. Once we kids were into something, they let it open more and more doors. I was never scolded for listening to Tigers' broadcasts well into the night. After the games I would usually travel the dial of clear channel AM radio that came alive in the dark, tuning in voices from throughout the country, or at least from east of the Mississippi. Sometimes there were other ballgames, but I gravitated to overnight talk shows. My favorite was the hilariously inventive Larry Glick, on Boston's WBZ.

Dad eventually dusted off his old multi-band radio and enlisted me in one of many home improvement adventures. This one involved the installation of an x-shaped antenna spanning the length of our 1960s ranch house, in the attic I had only ever heard about. Without masks and coughing in the dark from the dense fiberglass insulation, we hunted and fished to locate the spot and poke through my bedroom ceiling the wire that gave Dad's old short-wave receiver the boost it needed to become my ticket to the world. From then on it was the BBC World Service, Radio Moscow, and the Voice of America that narrated my dreams.

I never talked baseball with Dad, and never missed out because of it. We talked about the horizon and how to get there. He had used baseball to help me start to see what was ahead in life. My prowess on the diamond peaked in Little League, an era documented by Dad's photography and home movies. But in my mind I remain a legend on the softball field, and I am proud to recall that Dad and Mom, visiting when my wife and I lived in Washington, D.C., both witnessed one of my majestic home runs lofted into the trees along the National Mall during a congressional staffer league game.

I spent a few of my early career years in radio, and then in other areas of communications. I've been a somewhat restless adult, knowing that there is always something new to experience. As Dad and I both grew older, I turned to him less for guidance. His life lessons had become part of me.

It's always been a different story with Mom when it comes to baseball. We talk about the roles the game plays in life and its place in history. We don't talk statistics or name players by name, but we've often talked about great broadcasters. To this day, when she reads something interesting about baseball in the *Chicago Tribune*—her hometown paper for the past 30 years— it's clipped, folded into an envelope, and in my hands in a matter of days.

Thanks to Mom and Dad, baseball became a channel through which I grew to better understand and enjoy life. Our kids have grown with their own interests, but we have tried to instill the values and ideals that, for me, were amplified through my relationship with baseball. Be patient. Listen. Observe the world around you and watch the games within the game. Read. Know history. Love your parents. Build the future on encouragement.

And Go Tigers!

Finding Home
My Grandfather and
the House of David Baseball Team

JUANITA RAMSEY-JEVNE

They came seeking immortality. A few, including my grandfather and great-uncle, got it.

My sister pulled into a parking spot under the shade of a large tree and turned off the motor. We sat looking at the old brick buildings of the once thriving religious commune near Benton Harbor, Michigan. Both our maternal grandparents had been raised here. In exchange for the promise of being one of the select Tribes of Israel that would live forever in their human bodies and never die, their families had surrendered all their wealth and possessions and agreed to live according to the community rules, never cutting or shaving their hair, consuming no alcohol, tobacco or meat, using no profanity, and abstaining from sex. To ensure celibacy, the families had lived in separate male and female dormitories.

After a lifetime of hearing this improbable story, we had finally loaded our now 84-year-old mother into the car and driven from my sister's house in Indianapolis to visit what still remained of the commune. We were on a mission to sift the truth of our family history from the chaff of the hallucinations and paranoia of the mental illness Mom had suffered during our childhood. My son, William, came with us.

Now, despite the proof of the buildings in front of us, it was still difficult to accept that the House of David had been real.

"You know I never lived here," Mom said, from the back seat. "I just came here to meet my father when I was seventeen." After a moment she asked, "Whatever gave you the idea to come to the House of David?"

"Baseball," I answered.

A few years earlier, while looking for books to add to my fifth grade

78

class library, I had found *Finding Buck McHenry* by Alfred Slote, a baseball story that introduced me to the Negro Leagues of the early 20th century. In the fictionalized story, three kids create an overflow Little League team and need a coach. They find one in the long-time school janitor who apparently knows everything about the old Negro Leagues, and the limits imposed on these top-level players due to the fierce segregation of baseball.

Some students made posters of the teams: the Kansas City Monarchs, the Homestead Grays, the Indianapolis Clowns. Others reported on the players, young men transformed by talent and alchemical nicknames into baseball stars: Smokey Joe Williams, Cool Papa Bell, and the famous pitcher, Satchel Paige.

Mom had told us her father played baseball for the House of David, but as kids we couldn't tell if anything she said was true. After our father had died, we grew up alone in Joplin, Missouri, far from any relatives. Grandparents, aunts, uncles and cousins were less real to us than the voices—Mom called them the *Mean People*—whose strange rules controlled our lives. But during the book study, while researching the Negro Leagues, I had found proof that the House of David baseball team existed. Perhaps our grandfather had been a player.

At the small visitor's center, we learned there was a tour starting in the old barn. We pushed Mom's wheelchair inside as the first slide was projected on the screen. A man with a waist-length beard wearing a baseball cap over a long braid stopped in mid-sentence as we came in. He smiled. "You haven't missed too much. Join us."

To my surprise, before we sat down, Sylvia introduced Mom. "This is my mother Waneta Mae Vieritz. Her parents lived here. She is the daughter of Ora Mae Lynch and Arthur William Vieritz."

"Artie Vieritz! The ball player!" the man said excitedly. He seemed stunned.

I know we were.

For the first time in our lives, someone knew our family.

The bearded man rushed forward, knelt and took both of Mom's hands in his, pumping them up and down. "It is an honor to meet Artie's daughter! I'm Ron Taylor." He turned to the other tour goers and gestured to Mom. "Her father was one of the famous House of David ball players! You'll be hearing more about them during the slideshow." He wheeled Mom's chair to the front row and began the show again.

A picture appeared of a longhaired, bearded man wearing a white suit and white broad-brimmed hat standing next to a woman with long dark hair, wearing a high-collared, long-sleeved blouse and a floor-length skirt.

"This is Benjamin Purnell and his wife Mary, the founders of the Israelite House of David. They are the Seventh Prophets as foretold in the Book of

Revelations," announced Ron, his voice as matter-of-fact as if he were reading a grocery list.

After several more slides and an explanation of the beliefs and habits of the colony, he clicked on a picture of a long line of people walking down a street. "On March 25th, 1905, eighty-five Australians arrived in Benton Harbor to join the Israelite House of David, followed by another group in 1916.

Our grandfather had been one of those Australians.

Next was a panoramic photo of a large festive crowd of men, women and children dressed in their summer finery out for a day of entertainment at the Colony's amusement park. Two white horses with plumes on their heads were hitched one behind the other to a high-wheeled carriage that stood on a round center platform in the midst of the crowd.

Ron described the scene. "This photo was taken on August 10, 1919, at the Eden Springs Park in its 11th season of operation. They also had an ice cream parlor, a greenhouse, an aviary, a zoo, a baseball field, and a large auditorium that featured silent movies, theatre plays and Israelite preachers in public services. This was the premiere amusement park in this part of the country. At the same time, touring around the country, the baseball team was receiving national attention, for their long hair and because they were winning games and put on a great show. A few players invented a game called "pepper" in which the they fired the baseball from behind their backs or between their legs and concealed the ball inside their beards."

A sepia-toned slide of a group of young men in baseball uniforms with waist-length hair unbraided and on display filled the screen. "Here is the famous House of David Baseball Team," announced Ron. He walked to the screen. "And this," he said, lightly touching the image of the handsome young man in the center, "is your father, Artie Vieritz."

Mom was tired after the show. Ron directed us to the museum then led the rest of the group on the remaining stops of the tour. The large brick building that had originally been an auditorium was filled with photos, artifacts, and historical documents. Sylvia found the first prize. "Look! Here's Ora Mae!"

William called out next. "I found the baseball stuff!"

A large display of gloves, bats, balls, uniforms and other memorabilia spread over several tables. The walls were covered with publicity photos and playbills from the barnstorming tours. A large poster was prominently displayed. Words in black, blue and red marched down the center in various sizes. On the left was a large image of a tall, skinny Negro League player wound up for a pitch. It was Satchel Paige. He and his All Stars were on a tour with the House of David team. William and I both exclaimed. Sylvia walked over to see what was so exciting.

"It's Satchel Paige," I said. "I can't believe it!"

Sylvia smiled, then looked at the poster. On the right a bearded, long-haired House of David player was standing in position. He was crouched low, knees bent, torso twisted, arms raised high, the bat cocked and ready to swing. She leaned forward to read the name..

"Doc Tally, inventor of the famous 'Pepper Ball' exhibition." She nudged Mom. "Tally? Wasn't that Aunt Edith's last name?"

Mom roused herself and looked up. "That's Edith's husband."

All three of us turned and stared.

"Doc Tally is your uncle. By marriage." Mom dropped the bomb casually.

"Our uncle played with Satchel Paige?"

"Great-uncle actually," Mom corrected.

"Wow!"

William was impressed but puzzled. "Grandma," he said slowly, "if the men and women lived separately and were supposed to be..." he stopped for a moment, "celibate, then how was Doc Tally Edith's husband?"

Mom looked around then whispered. "There was a mass marriage. They lined up all the young people, paired them off and they were married."

"Why?" William asked, sounding as if the words "yuck" and "gross" and "that's awful" were trying to push out of his throat.

"They had to. Rumors were going around. The people in Benton Harbor didn't trust the House of David. All those young people living here and no one married?" she explained softly.

"And that's when your parents got married, too?"

"Sometime around then. I don't know the exact dates."

I had heard this story for years, but it was different now that we were actually here. What a strange life my relatives had lived.

Mom added, "It was difficult for Edith when her daughter Myrtle came along."

"I bet it was," I said softly. Even with loose dresses, a pregnancy was going to show some time.

"Edith said they weren't mean to her," Mom continued, "they just ignored her. They looked at her without really looking."

"Juanita, it's Art!" Sylvia was holding a sepia photograph in front of me. Our grandfather was posed in another team photo. Standing behind him was Doc Tally.

"Did your father go on the barnstorming tours?" I asked.

"Yes. He played for several years. Until he and my mother left the House of David." She paused. "He hated to give up baseball. He promised my mother if she married him he would take her away, but then he played another season. She never forgave him for that." Mom stared blindly at the posters. "When they left, they were given a one-way ticket to Ann Arbor and a five-dollar bill. The only job Art could find was sweeping streets. He wanted to come back just to work, but Ora Mae refused. They got divorced. He returned and played for the team again. Neither one of them knew she was pregnant. When I was born, she put me in an orphanage. Never told Art."

Two baseball players. One mass marriage. Two baby girls. One mother stayed and raised her child in the women's quarters. The other got away but had to put her child in an orphanage. Neither choice seemed very good.

"What was it like to meet your father?" Sylvia asked.

"Very nice. After my father got my letter, they sent me a reply and a ticket for the train. They wanted to meet me."

"He must have been surprised to find out he had another child."

"Yes, he was," Mom agreed. "But when I got here they were just as nice as could be. I was raised as an only child you know, and suddenly I had two half-sisters, and a stepmother, aunts, uncles, cousins. We met at his house at the dairy. But he brought me here to meet my aunts and my grandmother."

I looked around, trying to imagine what it would have been like in 1939. I looked at Mom, trying to imagine what it must have been like for her, a 17-year-old girl, coming alone to meet the father who hadn't even known she existed.

Ron Taylor walked up smiling. "I see you found the baseball section. Did you see the pictures of your father?"

Mom nodded.

"And we found out Doc Tally was her uncle," Sylvia told him. "He was married to Mom's Aunt Edith, Art's half sister."

"Wonderful," Ron said. "That's just wonderful."

Mom was clearly exhausted, but agreed to stop at the gift shop on our way out.

"Our tour was lovely," Sylvia told the woman at the counter. "We found lots of information about our family."

"Oh, I'm glad."

"Did you live here?" Sylvia asked. The woman shifted. Her smile seemed to lose some wattage.

"For a while, as a child," she finally said.

"Then I wonder if you knew our aunt? Edith Tally? She was married to Doc Tally?" Sylvia tilted her head. "And her daughter, Myrtle? She was our cousin."

After a pause, she slowly replied, "Yes, I knew them." She pointed out the tall window. "That was their room, right up there on the second floor."

The shop had copies of old photos for sale, especially the baseball teams. I selected pictures of our grandfather then noticed a small book with a sepia photo of the baseball team on the cover. The title was centered at the bottom of the photo: THE HOUSE OF DAVID BASEBALL TEAM. A young Doc Tally was in the second row, arms akimbo, hands at his waist. And sitting in the front row, as if he were holding the book title in his lap, his long blonde hair swept over his right shoulder, sat Artie Vieritz, my future grandfather looking out at me from our strange past.

I picked up the book, staring at the cover. Without even skimming it, I added five copies to my stack of photos. Then I walked over and knelt next to Mom's wheelchair. William joined me. I handed him the photos one at a time and he showed them to Grandma, his thick blonde hair so much like his great-grandfather's. I saved the book until the last.

"Sylvia, look at this," I said, wanting my entire audience paying attention for the big moment. I held the book in front of Mom.

"Your dad is on the cover of a book," I said, almost crying, and handed her a copy, then gave one to both William and Sylvia.

"Oh, my goodness," Sylvia said softly, gently turning the book over and over. "Oh, my goodness."

In the years to come, I would read the book many times, learning that the House of David Baseball Team had been one of the most popular barnstorming teams in the country. They made money for the colony and could pass out lots of literature. They played two or three games a day in a season that lasted over 150 days and traveled thousands of miles. There were few places on the map of my life they had not played. In 1933, they hired Jackie Mitchell to pitch, the first woman to sign a professional baseball contract. They were one of the first teams to integrate baseball, hiring Satchel Paige and his catcher, Cy Perkins, to help them win the *Denver Post* tournament in 1934. They toured for months with the Kansas City Monarchs and Satchel's All Stars. They hired Babe Didricksen to pitch a season. The home team played in their own ballpark in Benton Harbor. They were one of the first teams to use lights to play at night.

Our grandfather quit the circuit in the mid-twenties to marry again. I have found no baseball statistics for him yet. But our great-uncle, Jesse "Doc" Tally, has plenty. He arrived at the Colony in October of 1914 at age 18. The next year, he helped form the original baseball team, and would play his entire life, as a right-handed knuckleball pitcher and a left-handed-hitting outfielder. He barnstormed all over the country plus Mexico, Canada and Hawaii, playing with all the people mentioned above. In 1950, while preparing for his 36th season he died from "causes unknown."

The team was featured in many articles, including a 1920 New York Times pictorial. I would find Art and Doc Tally's pictures in articles in a 1970 feature in *Sports Illustrated*, a web article on an independent sports website, *The Classical*, and a 2013 article in the *Boston Globe*. The team got a cameo in Ken Burns' baseball documentary. Each time I found them, I teared up again. When I read an essay by baseball writer Roger Angell, I finally understood why: "[Baseball] is like joining an enormous family with ancestors and forebears and famous stories … and it's a privilege. It means a lot."

Back in the gift shop, William was reading the text. Mom was holding her book in her lap, a tired old lady. I realized she didn't understand our need for this pilgrimage. Mom had learned at 17 that she was part of a long lineage. We had been the nonbelievers. But finally here was proof.

Baseball is real. When a player walks up to the mound, life is reduced to the truth of a bat, a ball, a hit or a strike, safe or out. No matter the conflicting beliefs and confusion of the rest of life, in baseball one always knows the score.

"Mom, did I ever meet Art?" I asked as we pushed Mom to the car.

"Yes. He and his second wife came to visit us in Arkansas when you were about one," she said. "You were just learning to walk. They thought the shoes I had bought you would ruin your feet. So they went out to the Stride Rite shoe store and got you a new pair."

I let this new story sink in. Artie Vieritz, the one-time ball player, my grandfather, had bought me, his youngest granddaughter, my first pair of shoes. I smiled, happy to know he had met me. Happy to know he had cared.

I felt like I had just scored a home run.

What Is That Blue Man Doing?

Ellyn Ritterskamp

We used to get funny calls at my newspaper.

One of my favorites was during the Carolina Panthers' 2009 season, when DeAngelo Williams and Jonathan Stewart both rushed for over 1,000 yards for the same team. A caller wanted to know who was the first pair to have done that, and we tracked down Larry Csonka and Mercury Morris of the 1972 Dolphins (the other four pairs: Franco Harris and Rocky Bleier, Kevin Mack and Earnest Byner, Warrick Dunn and Michael Vick, and Brandon Jacobs and Derrick Ward).

Those were the easier calls to handle. The harder ones involved complaints: Which satellite channel was a game on ("check your onscreen guide"), or why didn't we have scores from a Hawaii golf tournament in the paper that morning (the answer required us to explain time zones).

A caller this season complained that the Atlanta Braves were not being aired on one of the several Fox Sports network stations that Sunday. My first answer was that the Braves were awful, but the longer answer is that broadcast television is free (in the sense that we pay for it by watching ads between innings). When a thing is free, it's a little tacky to complain about it—either accept the free thing, or don't. I encouraged him to look into the many ways he could buy access to an entire season of Major League Baseball, or just the Braves, or just a specific game.

I did not say what I'd been thinking, which was, "Get off your couch and go to a live game. It's so much better!"

When you're in the stands at a minor league game, you can see the whole field, not just the part the TV producer shows you. You can have conversations like this one, from around 1980 at a game between the Charlotte Os and the Memphis Chicks (the blue people):

85

Mom: What is that blue man doing?
Me: He's getting ready to try to steal second base.
Mom: Why is he wiggling like that?
Me: So he can take off when the pitcher comes set.
Mom: Why doesn't he just run now?
Me: Because they will throw him out.

I love that a game that represents the American way puts such a premium on a thing called "stealing." If you can steal second, you have a much better chance of scoring on the next hit. I also love that so much of what's fun about baseball is the anticipation: watching that wiggling, wriggling base runner, holding our breath while he decides when to take off, clenching our teeth as he arrives at second base along with the throw from the catcher ... there's not much else like this sequence for me in sport.

A friend once asked me why I like baseball so much—he prefers hockey and basketball. I said, "Your sports are basically fluid, and mine is basically static, but you never know when it's going to *become* fluid." That anticipation aspect is the difference.

The blue man, the Memphis base runner, had gone into the shuffling, twitching, side-to-side rocking motion that is unique to base runners and to tennis players awaiting serve. He wanted to be able to run to second base as the pitcher delivered, but also to be ready to return to first base if the pitcher tried to throw him out.

Mom's questions about stealing were valid. I tried to explain the notion of a balk, in which the pitcher has failed to pause long enough to give the runner his fair chance. Balks are just goofy, especially when a game ends on one. But that explanation led me to this one: Baseball is weird in that we don't have proportional punishment. We have either ejection from the game, or nothing. The umpire returns things to where they were, or ejects a player. There's nothing in between.

Most other sports have a medium penalty: we toss you in the box, or push your team back 10 yards, or tag you with a foul. Baseball players either get away with an infraction or they get tossed, with no middle ground. Since the punishment is so drastic, umps tend not to invoke it unless they've been personally insulted. They can't assess a one-strike penalty or send a runner backward one base, or dock the team an additional out. The game would be so different if they could do any of these!

Because baseball doesn't have punitive punishments, it's rather tolerant of minor infractions, policing away the ones that are most obvious, and overlooking those that are more craftily carried out. The system works relatively well. The game doesn't disintegrate into chaos because the players and managers have an unwritten code of conduct.

There are pitchers who doctor the ball—if they aren't caught, they get away with it and have a decent outing. If they're caught, they still get a warning.

Baseball parks have minimum conditions that must be met, but there are plenty of alterations that go on beyond these minimums. Some are legal. Some are not. A groundskeeper for a team with a pitcher who has a special kind of slide-step may rake the dirt a particular way on the pitcher's mound, just that day. Managers of pitchers who induce lots of ground balls might ask their grounds crew to cut the grass a bit shorter or higher based on that pitcher's tendencies. The mowing job can be tailored to the players the manager starts that day, as the height of the grass can affect the speed of the ball. These alterations are only quasi-legal, but since all teams want to be able to make them, seldom does anyone complain about an opponent's tweakings.

We don't just steal bases—we steal signs. Base coaches signal batters about strategy and catchers signal pitchers what to throw. Opponents try to intercept these signals, so they'll know what's coming. Here's the fun part: there's nothing in the rules about signaling. A team is free to play with no signals, if it likes. Most teams change their signals from catcher to pitcher when there's a runner on second, because the runner can see the signals and could warn the batter.

The trouble comes when players or managers catch the signs of the other team and use them. An Atlanta hitter some years back was accused of this. He did hit rather well against that team, so maybe he did figure out their signs. The response to this is simple, though: he broke no rules. If he catches a sloppily executed series of signals, he deserves the good result.

I've read that Bobby Thomson's Giants had stolen the catcher's signs from the Dodgers in 1951—that's how he knew what Ralph Branca would throw on his home run that won the pennant. In a Wall Street Journal article in 2001, Thomson said they did have the signs, but that he didn't get that one.

When you think someone has your signals, the solution is to change to a different batch. Since there are no written rules about signaling systems, there can be no cheating. We cannot break a law that doesn't exist.

Or can we? Unwritten laws carry a lot of weight. There are plenty of occasions, over the course of a season, for a bending of this rule to balance out the tweaking of that one. Most smaller infractions are overlooked; everyone knows that a true bad apple will get what he or she deserves.

It's in our smaller, cheaper, local parks that all of this gets played out so many days over the summer. My friend who learned much of what he knows about baseball from his sister, 75 years ago, said they went to a game and he heard the announcer at the end of an inning: No runs, no hits, no errors. He said to his sister, "I know I saw one of those men hit the ball!" That's how he learned that a hit means something particular. Words mean things, though sometimes they mean esoteric things.

He also thought a third-base coach was having a medical problem, the first time he saw one giving signals to the hitter.

My favorite moment of explaining the game came last season, after the Charlotte Knights had recently returned to downtown Charlotte after having played literally in another state for 24 seasons. I took my friend to a day game, where we wallowed in the sunshine. As the Knights took the field for the first pitch, she surveyed the situation and said she believed things would go better if they "put a couple more men out there."

Maybe we are spoiled where I live, by having so many minor league teams within driving distance. After having visited all the major league parks over 20 years or so, I've been able to visit all of the South Atlantic parks in one season—at 14 teams, that does take some planning.

Another summer, my mom and I toured the Carolina League, which has eight teams but only three in the Carolinas. Our local team is in the International League, but that's just too spread out to tackle the whole thing in one summer.

Every single one of those games was a better experience than 90 percent of the games I've seen on TV. Those other 10 percent are all playoff games, so they're in a different category anyway.

There are a bunch of different things you get in the minors: goofy team names, weird foods and bizarre mascots. Where else will you find the Boll Weevils, Sand Gnats or Blue Rocks?

Besides a state fair, you don't eat most of these anywhere—and that's probably a good thing: Peanut butter and jelly doughnut (Lexington Legends); deep fried Moon Pies (Asheville Tourists); Sweenie Donut Dog with raspberry jam and bacon (Wilmington Blue Rocks); Swamp Dog, with shrimp and grits on top (Delmarva Shorebirds).

At the top of my mascot list is the Wilmington Blue Rocks (Delaware), who have three. Rocky Bluewinkle (a moose) and Rubble (a giant blue rock) are there most of the time, while Mr. Celery dances behind home plate only when the home team hits a home run.

Muddy the Mudcat may be the least attractive mascot I've seen—he's a catfish representing the Carolina Mudcats. The cutest mascot in our area is easily Miss Lou Lou Gehrig, a now-retired bat dog for the Greensboro Grasshoppers.

Minor League ball also gave Mom and me our chance to sing together in public. We braved chicken-bone throwing fans behind home plate to sing "O, Canada" and "The Star-Spangled Banner" for the Charlotte Knights, when they played in Fort Mill, South Carolina. The International League included the Ottawa Lynx back then—now it's not even international anymore. That is such a sweet anthem, and so much easier to sing than our own. I know nowadays we are re-examining the lyrics to our anthem, especially the third and fourth verses of the source poem, and that's good. Words mean things. But for this song, in particular, the notes and chords themselves are what move me.

Baseball and singing run in our family. During those early-'80s games at Crockett Park in Charlotte, my dad's mother was the first to stand when they said, "Please join us in singing our national anthem." She had classical training and was not shy about letting it rip, but as kids, we didn't appreciate her talent because we were cringing at everyone in the park looking our way when she sang.

In those summers in the 1980s in Charlotte, we didn't appreciate what we were getting to see with Cal Ripken, Jr., and Billy Ripken, who got most of the attention. I also remember an outfielder named Drungo LaRue Hazewood, whose name rang out for so long when the announcer called him, it echoed from somewhere. Haaaaaaaaaaaaaaze—wooooood. He had run to his place in center by the time his name stopped echoing.

We know how it turned out for the Ripkens. Hazewood had a cup of coffee with the parent Orioles in 1980 but like so many, couldn't hit a curve. He died a few years ago at age 53. Some dust got in my eye and made it water a little bit that day. One of the things we treasure about baseball is the way it connects us to our past. When he died, I was 13 again for a moment, sitting in the sun and listening to my grandmother sing.

It took me years to figure out the main thing I love about baseball. I had worked out that I appreciate that it's relatively non-violent, and that it gives us time to anticipate what might happen, and that there is no clock.

The terrorist attacks on September 11 brought baseball into focus for me. We spent a week without games after the planes crashed, and that was right. The first night the games returned, I watched the highlights show late at night, and none of the images were of the game being played: they were of people in the stands, singing, praying, and just being together.

It reminded us who we were, and who we are. Baseball reminded us that there's always the next out, or the next inning, or if our game does finally end, there's always next year.

Baseball gave us a place to sit together. It gave us hope.

Dark as a Dungeon
Coal Country Baseball

JODY DIPERNA

Cumberland "Cum" Posey is one of just eighteen Negro Leagues ball-players enshrined in the Baseball Hall of Fame. A tremendous fielder and base runner, Posey was a titan in black baseball. When he hung up his spikes, he proved to be an even better owner than he was a left fielder. He made his Homestead Grays a perennial powerhouse and one of the few consistently solvent barnstorming units in the nation.

But on this day in 1920, Posey was a 30-year-old ballplayer standing on second base, his team locked in a 1–1 tie. Posey looked out at the trees beyond the players' benches and at Chestnut Ridge beyond that. Silvery smoke from the coking oven hung in the air. Behind him, beyond the limits of the outfield, fans picnicked and played cards and passed the bottle. They filled the small bleachers, too, taking in the sport that was an obsession in mining towns like this. For the men for whom this was their day off from the mines and the coke ovens, it was that rare chance to socialize and relax, out of doors, in the sunshine and fresh air.

There were a fair number of black fans in attendance, too. Some had made the trip from Pittsburgh to see their Grays. But others were from patches and towns all around Connellsville. It was a rare chance for them to see a great black ball club. A Saturday ballgame was always a festive occasion. It was the biggest crowd of the season at Fayette Field.

Then the strangest balk call anyone ever saw advanced Posey to third base.

But perhaps I should back up and tell you about these teams, the Home-stead Grays and the Connellsville Independents. Maybe I should tell you about these baseball-mad towns in the heart of western Pennsylvania's coal region.

This unassuming collection of hill towns is where Henry Clay Frick built his empire and the origin of the coal and coke that fired Andrew Carnegie's steel mills, the greatest steel operation the world has ever seen. In the summer of 1920, there were nearly 35,000 beehive ovens blazing, about half of those Frick Co. ovens, all producing Pittsburgh coke, a product that could do the heavy lifting of firing the blast furnaces used to make steel. Into those thousands and thousands of beehives, the cokers fed more than 18 million tons of coal. They produced more than 12 million tons of coke in just 1920 alone.

Built along both sides of the Youghiogheny River about 50 miles south of Pittsburgh, Connellsville sits in the westernmost ridge of the Appalachian Mountains. Chestnut Ridge dominates as far as the eye can see. As much as the river and the mountains shaped the area, the bituminous coal deep underneath transformed it. The Connellsville coke region is 25 miles long and two and one-half miles wide, loaded with Pittsburgh coal.

As deep as 650 feet underground, miners and tunnelers laid in puddles picking and setting charges, sorting and shoveling coal. They often worked in tandem and sometimes in small groups. Others in the mines, like the nippers, worked in extreme isolation, in pitch-blackness, with no light but that of their carbide lamps. They all lived most of their waking hours, most of their lives, facing their own mortality: everyone knew men who died in random accidents, in cave-ins, in explosions, and from deadly gas.

Underneath, the miners worked in the chill dark, while up top the cokers labored in the face of unimaginably intense conflagrations. It was their job to feed and tend the brick beehive ovens built in long stretches into the Appalachian hillsides. When a battery of ovens—heated with charcoal and coal—was hot enough, a charger came through. He would empty a charge of five tons of coal into the blazing oven through the tunnel head, the hole at the top. The leveler took over from there, spreading the coal out evenly with a toothless rake about 15 feet long, while the oven blazed like all the furies of hell. When he was done with one, he moved on down the battery, to the next oven, and the next, and the next.

A mason would brick up the oven, leaving a small opening for attendants who regulated the burns over several days. When the coke was ready, a puller would open the door and quench the finished coke with a hose. Then he'd break up the coke with an iron bar and pull it out. Using fork like shovels to sift out impurities, more men carefully loaded the coke into wheelbarrows and wagons for transport.

The burning coke gave off a strong, disagreeable smell. The ovens lit up the sky at night—high noon or midnight, the sky had a similar grayish hue. The soot from Pittsburgh coke was lustrous silver and it covered everything. The winds along Chestnut Ridge are powerful and they carried silvery cinders from the batteries into homes, into businesses, into the riverbed, into any crack or crevice it could find. Coke burns were impossible to escape.

Working miners and cokers lived in company houses in patches near the mine or the oven batteries. They were at the behest of the company every moment of every day and going on strike or even talking union often meant immediate eviction, usually at gunpoint by company guards.

Long dangerous days for scant pay, they and their families lived lives on the margins of scarcity. Wives cultivated prized food gardens on the hillsides. Everybody lived on a hill—there just wasn't that much flat land around. Even with the gardens, many days passed where dinner was coffee soup (black coffee with bread) or tatties and yolly bread (potatoes and bread with jelly) for dinner.

It was hard for folks to escape the industry and the long reach of the company. How could you forget, even for a moment, with the night skies lit like a biblical battle, cinders in every drawer and nook, and the smell, an entire county suffused with the acrid smell of rotten eggs? But the patch residents *could* escape for a few hours of respite watching and playing baseball. America's pastime was wildly popular in the coal district and the area was littered with teams.

In the early going days, mining and coking companies often sponsored teams. To be the sheltering hand that provided both work and leisure, it was welfare capitalism at its finest, an effort to bind workers to the company. The Frick Coke Company had teams in all of their patches, places like Trotter, Monarch, Leisenring, Davidson, Morgan, Bute, Bitner and Lemont. The rivalries between company teams were organic, bitter and intense. In the summer of 1920, Trotter and Leisenring played a five-game series, each of which drew no fewer than 1,500 fans, and one that drew as many as 3,000 spectators.

The miners and cokers were immigrants and the sons of immigrants, mostly from southern and eastern Europe. They were also native born. Some were African Americans who left sharecropping as part of the great migration; others were the descendants of Welsh miners who came to this part of coal country several generations earlier. Baseball was where they all came to life, where they felt a part of the American dream, and where they became fully American.

*   *   *

The Yough runs right through Connellsville flowing north into the Monongahela River. Andrew Carnegie built his colossus steel works on the banks of the Mon, just on the other side of the river from the City of Pittsburgh. Though Major League Baseball was accessible to fans willing to travel just a few miles, community baseball filled most days here, like the coke country that fed it. The Steel Works League pitted teams from various shops in the works (Open Hearth, Electric, Armor, Plate and so on) against one another. Just an eight-team league, they filled out their schedules with teams outside the Works, independent community teams, mostly white, and also against the black Homestead Grays team.

While black ballplayers were barred from the Major Leagues, they were also, by and large, barred from playing for white teams at any level. Integration simply was not done. But competition between white teams and black teams was acceptable, at least in the industrial north. In the south, custom and Jim Crow made games between white and black teams dangerous rarities.

Black teams were scattered all over the nation. A team would form and then dissolve and a new team would crop up in its place. It was hard going, financially. Sometimes there was a "colored world series." Sometimes not. The champion was loosely decided. But some teams had real staying power and in Chicago in the summer of 1920, Rube Foster established the first lasting black league, the Negro National League, which included Foster's own Chicago American Giants, as well as six other Midwestern teams. Foster's league was the first step toward real hierarchical structure to parallel the white Major Leagues.

The Grays, of course, went on to become one of the storied teams in the history of Negro Leagues Baseball, but at this point, they were a team unaffiliated with any league, scraping by to cover their bills. Among both black and white sandlotters, they had a reputation as one of the best teams around. Built on great pitching and speed, their opening game in May of 1920 drew more than 3,000 to see them defeat the (white) Homestead Independents.

Baseball may be a game, a pastoral balm in harsh industrial times, but it is also a business, especially for a black ball club in 1920 driven by harsh economic exigencies. Dependent on gate receipts to stay afloat financially, the Grays scheduled wisely, but often anywhere that could provide them with a good audience. And so they scheduled a match with the Connellsville Independents.

For weeks, the *Connellsville Daily Courier* trumpeted the match up with the Grays. The appetite for baseball was great, but many locals were more loyal to their respective patch teams with established, bitter rivalries like the one between Trotter and Leisenring rating No. 1. Folks with so little disposable income, and even less leisure time, were a hard sell for the new town team. It required spectacle, something they couldn't see otherwise. The Grays, the "fastest colored baseball team in the country," were just such a drawing card.

Fayette Field sat on one of the rare flat stretches of ground in the area. Most of the living and working and dying took place on the hillsides, with the flat land reserved for the baseball diamond. Still, the field was rugged. When Cum Posey arrived a few days in advance of the game, he insisted the field be overhauled. The most egregious holes and ruts in the infield were filled and leveled. A reaper was taken to the outfield grass. Neighborhood boys moved through to pick big stones off the diamond.

As always in Connellsville, the skies had that ineffable grayish hue, with cinders dusting the trees and that omnipresent rotten egg smell. Still, game day was a perfect day for baseball, in the mid–'80s with few clouds.

Miners and nippers, levelers and chargers, masons and pullers, came from their company homes in the patches named for the coal and coke operations all around. They came from Adelaide and Leith, Rist and Brinkerton, Dorothy, Edenborn and Tip Top.

When coal first started being mined in the area in the 1880s, the population was around 3,500. In 1920, close to 16,000 people populated Connellsville. Maybe Paul Koneval, a coker who worked for the Frick Company and his neighbor, Mary Slifka, who had one of the most enviable, abundant gardens in Smock were at Fayette Field? Perhaps Paul Frederick, a coke leveler at the Standard works paid his 50 cents for entry. Charles Newman, an African American janitor may have come to see the famous colored nine. They all made their way to witness the "biggest and most attractive baseball game ever arranged to be played in this city," per the Connellsville daily.

Certainly not in attendance on that summer day was a 19-year-old miner from Dunbar whose head was blown off by an explosion in the mines two weeks prior. Neither was John J. Slacker, Jr., a worker at the Marion Coal & Coke Company whose body was found cut into many pieces along the track between the company's mine and coke plant after he had fallen under some machinery. John Edwards, 20, was not there, having been smothered in a slate-fall deep underground. Nor was J. H. Zorn, a foreman with the United States Bureau of Mines who was overcome by noxious gas while leading a rescue to unearth the bodies of nine men entombed after an explosion in the Union Collieries.

Ah, to move in the open, in the green spaces, in the fresh air and the sunshine. To move freely, rather than working, lying in puddles or hunched over. To feel the cool grass, rather than the heat of hell on earth. To spend just a few hours away from work to watch a baseball game. In mine towns and patches and camps all through the Appalachian coalfield, black diamonds were the engine of economic life, but baseball was life.

Aggressive base running was the calling card of the Grays and they delivered in the top of the first. Walker hit a high hopper over third base for a single, and then stole second. When Pearson hit sharply to third, Walker was already on the run, racing around to score. Connellsville tied it up with back-to-back doubles in the third inning, and there the matter stood until the balk call.

The teams had agreed to provide one official each. The umpire hired by the Grays ruled that Connellsville catcher Tom Jones was outside the batter's box when he threw out Posey stealing third. Clouding the matter further, he was also the brother of Cum Posey. It was, in the words of one reporter, a case of "blood being thicker than water."

The home team was furious. The Connellsville nine screamed that the fix was in. Posey said that if they were unhappy with the call, his team would leave with the game unfinished in the sixth inning. It was a stalemate, but Posey already had his share of the gate receipts. Still, he was loath to forfeit and disappoint fans. He reasoned that it was better for both clubs to continue and eventually, his argument won out.

Some in the crowd questioned the decision by the home club to continue. Many of the men were drunk—even though this was the first summer of Prohibition, miners always seemed to have some home brew to share, or knew how to lay their hands on some moonshine, or who had some bootleg liquor to sell. A Saturday ballgame meant drinking and the 21st Amendment could take the hindmost. Fans who had made bets on the Independents felt truly aggrieved. But mostly, they just wanted to see more baseball, so they settled back into the game.

When play resumed, the home team was rattled. The Grays put on a double steal. Pearson was picked off at first but first baseman Sam Labiak's throw to home sailed well past the catcher's head and into the trees. Posey scored easily. Another fielding error allowed the Grays to score two more.

In the last four frames, the Independents got some hits off Grays twirler Lefty Williams, but he always worked his way out of jams without giving up a run, preserving the 4–1 win for Homestead.

Though the outcome of the game was unsatisfying for the Independents, it served its purpose and they began drawing more and more fans. They even scheduled a re-match with the Grays in early September, hoping to settle the score. The Grays won that match easily, with no controversies.

The Independents gained fans as the season wore on and the Grays had a fantastic season, which they finished off by besting the Chicago American Giants in a match at Forbes Field, home of the Pittsburgh Pirates.

The Homestead Grays are gone now. So, too, are the Connellsville Independents. Fayette Field is a high school track. Connellsville is a shell of what it was during the boom years for coke. Fans follow baseball, but they follow the Pirates, not community teams.

You can still find vestiges of what it once was, though. You can still find some of the old company houses. If you're adventurous and willing to trespass, you can still find beehive ovens, crumbling and repatriated by nature. If you get really lucky, you may even find one of the old baseball fields, the vestiges of the prized diamond overgrown with weeds and grasses, home plate poking it's head out and a slight rise where the pitcher stood, while working men escaped for a few hours a week.

Pete Rose Way

L.C. FIORE

Pete Rose Way follows the Ohio River, past new condominiums and Yeatman's Cove, before flushing into Great American Ballpark, home of the Cincinnati Reds.

Peter Edward Rose is a native son, raised on the city's West Side. He was a 17-time All-Star, three-time World Series Champion, Most Valuable Player, and Rookie of the Year. He owns the record for the most career hits: 4,256. And in 1989, he was banned from the game for life, for betting on baseball.

Almost 30 years later, Pete Rose Way remains.

What you'll hear around Cincy, of course, if you ask even the most casual baseball fan, is that while Rose bet on baseball, he never bet against himself. For citizens of the Queen City, and Reds fans in general, this changes the color of the crime. If he never bet against himself, he never had reason to throw a game. Any gambler worth his salt would never have taken those odds anyway. "Charlie Hustle" played in more winning games than any player, ever: 1,972.

Growing up in a town that named a major right-of-way for an athlete before his career was finished, and then refused to change the name of the street after that athlete had been found guilty of basically the worst crime you can commit as a ballplayer, can't help but affect your point of view. Nationally there are strong feelings on both sides of the issue of whether Rose should one day be inducted into the Major League Baseball Hall of Fame. For me, like most Cincinnatians, the answer is clear: of course he should. Ty Cobb claimed to have killed a man, for Christ's sake, or so the legend goes, and he's got a plaque in Cooperstown.

For more or less my entire life, I've driven a route named after my hometown's biggest hero. He isn't the prettiest guy or the smoothest talker. He hit singles, which aren't very sexy. And even after admitting all the gambling

96

allegations were true, he's unrepentant. And yet. Driving to the ballpark, listening to the pre-game on 700 WLW, I wonder about that gray area between right and wrong and how we choose to remember not only players and celebrities, but one another.

After all, as someone once said, if you're not cheating, you're not trying hard enough. Baseball has a strange ethos where it's considered bad sportsmanship to cheat, but even worse sportsmanship to complain about the other guy cheating.

In Game 2 of the 2006 World Series, Detroit Tigers starting pitcher Kenny Rogers hurled an eight-inning shutout against St. Louis. The Cardinals grumbled that Rogers was doctoring the ball with pine tar; television cameras revealed a suspect macule on his pitching hand. The Gambler claimed it was only dirt and resin, and strictly legal.

This event recalled the New York Mets' Wally Backman, who, 20 years earlier in the National League Championship Series, accused opposing starting pitcher Mike Scott, of Houston, of scuffing baseballs. Scott had just thrown a complete game, allowing one run. In the clubhouse after, Backman produced seventeen balls allegedly altered by Scott.

In both cases, there was a universal shrug. From fans, from the media, from players.

"Everybody uses pine tar," said Boston's David Ortiz, in 2014. There'd been a kerfuffle during that day's game, about a suspect brown smudge on the neck of Michael Pineda, the Yankee pitcher. "No big deal."

In other words, no one likes a tattletale.

Lather one side of a baseball with moisture, or scrape it up real good, and you can control which direction the ball breaks. Or, lube the baseball, grip it so your fingers don't touch the seams, and let the ball squirt out of your hand, a process which removes just about all the spin and makes the ball behave a bit like what we know today as the splitter (see: almost every pitch Mariano Rivera ever threw).

Officially, you're not supposed to doctor the ball. The MLB rulebook states, "No player shall intentionally discolor or damage the ball by rubbing it with soil, rosin, paraffin, licorice, sand-paper, emery-paper, or other foreign substance." But Major League Baseball has always been a bit conflicted over the enforcement of this rule.

The spitter wasn't officially banned until 1919, and even then, each team could carry two designated spitball pitchers. After the 1920 season, the "shine ball" was banned league-wide, except for seventeen pitchers who were grandfathered in, including Hall of Famers Stan Coveleski, "Red" Faber, and Burleigh Grimes, who'd retire in 1934 as the last legal spitballer.

Ray Lyle "Pick" Fisher, who was among those spitball pitchers grandfathered in, after a 10-year career in which he won 100 games, was banned from baseball for life before the 1921 season over what appears to be a clerical error. The last team he pitched for was the Cincinnati Reds.

Today, pitchers continue to shine or scuff baseballs with all manner of products: pine tar, Vaseline, nail files. Perhaps licorice, still. Sometimes catchers do the honor and cut grooves into the ball on their shin guards or masks. Most of the time, they get away with it.

Gaylord Perry, winner of 314 games and a Hall of Famer, was a notorious spitballer, long after the pitch was declared illegal. He never denied it: in fact, he freely admitted it. This transparency was enough, apparently, for sportswriters to overlook the "character" clause on their Hall of Fame ballots and vote Perry in. The title of his autobiography? *Me and the Spitter.*

Batters cheat too. They cheat in little ways, like rubbing out the white lines of the batter's box so they can scoot a little bit further back, to allow themselves a little more time to see the pitch.

They cheat in big ways, like Yankee third baseman Graig Nettles, who broke his bat during a game in 1974, and six rubber balls went spraying across the infield. (Nonplussed, the catcher waltzed out and calmly picked them all up.) A bat that has been hollowed out and filled with rubber is lighter, allowing the hitter to be quicker on his swing and gain a millisecond advantage. In baseball, every millisecond counts.

In a July 1983, game against the Yankees, Kansas City's George Brett smashed a go-ahead home run but was subsequently called out when New York manager Billy Martin objected to the amount of pine tar on Brett's bat, which exceeded the eighteen-inch limit set by MLB. Brett went nuts, charging out of the dugout to argue—it's an iconic photo. Less well known is that the Royals later appealed that game and won. American League President Lee MacPhail declared the spirit of the pine tar rule was economics: in early baseball, they didn't want a bunch of sticky tree sap getting all over the balls. Baseballs were expensive back then. So he ruled that Brett gained no advantage by having too much pine tar on his bat and overturned the umpire's decision to call Brett out.

Basically, MacPhail agreed Martin was just being a tattletale, and let the home run stand.

(Here again we come across infamous spitballer Gaylord Perry, who knew a thing or two about flagrantly breaking rules: after Brett had been called out, in the ensuing scrum, Perry, who was then pitching for the Royals, hustled the illegal bat into the dugout and handed it off to a bat boy. The kid sprinted into the clubhouse with New York City policemen on his heels, trying to get rid of the bat before it could be confiscated as evidence and taken to the American League front office. Perry might have been a lot of things, but he wasn't dumb. Along with an unhittable spitter, he possessed a quick and brilliant criminal mind.)

* * *

Growing up long before the Internet, a friend and I ran our own fantasy baseball league. Two teams: his and mine. We drafted players, set our lineups each night, and dutifully recorded the accumulated stats in our individual Mead notebooks when they appeared in the paper the next day. We lived across town from one another, so we called each morning to see how the other guy's team had scored. What we should have done, in retrospect, was set our lineups before the first pitch. We might have even tracked one another's stats, instead of our own, to keep us honest. But hey, we were 10.

One night, Reds outfielder Max Venable, he of a .647 career OPS (on-base percentage plus slugging average), went one for four with a three-run bomb. The next morning, I retroactively slid him into my lineup. "You never start Venable!" my friend shouted through the phone. Was he accusing me of cheating? "I did last night," I told him. But Max Venable, while a personal favorite of mine, was no one's definition of a starter in a two-team fantasy baseball league. I'd cheated. Flagrantly. And yes, I did it all the time.

So did my friend: I just had enough class not to call him out on it.

* * *

Catchers may don the tools of ignorance, but they're as guilty as everyone else: they stomp on hitters' toes as they scamper out of the batter's box; they try to snag the ball mid-flight before the batter can make contact.

Since we've begun tracking catcher pitch-framing, it's become clear catchers can affect the outcome of balls and strikes with subtle turns of their wrists, by setting up correctly over the plate. The best catchers make the umpire think the pitch was a strike, even if it wasn't. In 2015, the Pirates' Francisco Cervelli turned over 200 pitches thrown out of the strike zone into strikes, by far the most in baseball. Deft glove work, or criminal subterfuge? Either way, some catchers are markedly better at it than others.

* * *

There's this myth that popular culture loves a comeback story. We actually tend to remember one another for our biggest failures.

Bill Buckner was a professional hitter, an All-Star and batting champion who played 22 years in the bigs. He was the first baseman for the Boston Red Sox when they met the New York Mets in the 1986 World Series. At that point, the Red Sox hadn't won a championship since 1918, suffering under "The Curse of the Bambino."

Game 6, with the Red Sox up three games to two, Buckner let a dribbler go through his legs for what should have been the final out. The Red Sox lost, and then went on to lose Game 7. Buckner received death threats until 2004, when the Red Sox finally won a championship. Mention him today, of course, and the image of him lumbering toward the line, the ball shooting beneath his glove into right field, is the first thing, and possibly the only thing, folks remember.

Fred Merkle was a nineteen-year-old backup first baseman for the New York Giants when they took on the Chicago Cubs for the 1908 pennant. In the first game he ever started, Merkle found himself as the runner coming from first for what should have been the pennant-clinching hit. In the on-field excitement, he failed to touch second base as the winning run scored, before presumably leaping onto the celebratory dog-pile. The Cubs appealed, Merkle was called out, the run was erased, and the Cubs eventually won the game—and the pennant. Merkle would go on to play 16 seasons, receiving MVP votes in 1911 and 1912. But mention his name today, and most everyone will shrug and say, "Merkle's Boner."

It's not only in baseball, of course. Names like Rod Blagojevich, Bill Cosby, Bernie Madoff, make us shake our heads with regret. Surely there's nothing to admire in these men—for posterity or otherwise?

A city like Cincinnati, which refuses to change the name of a street whose namesake has unrepentantly broken century-old rules, directs our hearts, perhaps, to some greater truth. While our failures should be acknowledged, and criminals should be punished for their crimes, perhaps our shortcomings should not define us. Or not entirely. And certainly not for eternity.

Pete Rose Way is a reminder that our failures make us human. Or maybe it's just that, in Cincinnati, we prefer our heroes flawed.

But every hero is flawed. Perhaps it's a little bit insane for us to make heroes out of athletes, whose only gift, let's be honest, is having exceedingly rare physical skills. Perhaps one day we'll appreciate their ability to swing a round bat at a round ball and hit it square, without demanding moral and ethical perfection as well.

Rose broke the letter of the law. He bet on baseball. George Brett broke the letter of the law too, but his home run stood. The difference is, perhaps, in one's perspective. In my darker moments, I wonder if the difference is politics, or likeability, or, as a lifelong and oft-neglected fan of Midwest sports, just good old-fashioned anti-fly-over-state bias.

Pete Rose Way originates in a part of Cincinnati once known as The Bottoms. In colonial times, it was where you got off your flatboat and went into town to get drunk and eat a hot meal. Later, in the early twentieth century, it was all tenements and industry, nowhere you'd want to find yourself after dark.

Now there are plans to build luxury condominiums there, and fancy shops, and the area has been rebranded as The Banks. The mayor lobbied hard and installed his streetcar that today runs from The Banks north into a rapidly gentrifying section of downtown, where restaurants sell hipster fried chicken and local microbrews.

In a real sense, Pete Rose Way now leads from the bottom to the one-percent, a true rags-to-riches story—the embodiment of the American Dream.

And when I drive Pete Rose Way, I don't think about criminality or banishment. Instead, I feel hopeful that I still have a chance to be remembered not for my biggest mistake, but for my successes—as small and insignificant as they might turn out to be.

How Gus Greenlee,
Sonnyman Jackson
and the Numbers Barons
Saved Black Baseball

KEVIN KIRKLAND

An ageless right arm and a ferocious short swing made Satchel Paige and Josh Gibson great. But millions of nickel bets and two nervy numbers bankers made them and their Pittsburgh teams legends.

A.W. "Gus" Greenlee and Rufus "Sonnyman" Jackson bankrolled the Pittsburgh Crawfords and Homestead Grays, two Western Pennsylvania powerhouses that alternately dominated organized black baseball in the 1930s and '40s.

Like many of their players, the two Southerners were part of the great African American migration to Northern industrial cities in the first half of the 20th century, Greenlee from Marion, North Carolina, Jackson from Columbus, Georgia. They worked menial jobs—Greenlee shined shoes, worked in a steel mill and bootlegged liquor from a taxicab during Prohibition. Then they discovered the numbers racket, also known as the policy game.

The Great Depression didn't faze Greenlee, who was reputed to make $20,000–$25,000 a day on his three-digit illegal lottery in the early 1930s. Numbers employed more than 500 people, most of them "runners" who stopped at each home, office, store and factory, collecting numbers and bets as small as a penny.

Greenlee's territory was the Hill District, Homewood, Garfield and the North Side—Pittsburgh's black neighborhoods. Proceeds came back to Greenlee and his partner, William "Woogie" Harris, at the Crawford Grill, a nightclub Greenlee owned in the Hill District. Jackson controlled the game in Homestead and nearby towns in the Monongahela River Valley south of Pittsburgh. He owned a club, too, the Skyrocket Cafe.

The winning number was usually the last three digits of a stock index in the morning newspaper. Greenlee paid off hits at 500 or 600 to 1, so a penny bet could net a player $5 or $6—enough for a nice dinner, a show and drinks afterward during the Depression.

Most blacks and many working-class whites discovered numbers in the mid–1920s. Many continued to play even after the Pennsylvania Lottery hijacked their game in the 1970s (the bankers' odds were better and no taxes!). Elijah "Lucky" Miller, a Homestead steelworker and Grays batboy in the 1930s and '40s, played numbers for most of his life. He died in 2010 at age 104.

"A nickel and nothing more," recalled his daughter, Ruth Hines of Wilkinsburg. "He won quite a bit. If you hit, you always tipped the runner a few dollars."

Multiply Lucky's nickels (and bigger bets) by millions and you get a glimpse of Greenlee and Jackson's fortunes in a time when any man with a job — black or white—was considered lucky. But why invest it in a black baseball team?

* * *

Long before Jackie Robinson broke the Major League color barrier in 1947, blacks were being paid to play baseball. The first all-black professional team formed in the 1860s and by the 1880s, the highlight of the social calendar in many black communities was doubleheaders on the anniversary of the Emancipation Proclamation and the Fourth of July.

In 1884, Moses "Fleet" Walker played catcher for the Toledo Blue Stockings, a white pro team in the American Association. A few other black ballplayers lasted a season or two in the white minor leagues, but soon the color line hardened and African Americans were forced to organize their own leagues or play in segregated industrial leagues.

In June 1922, the *Pittsburgh Courier* reported the opening of the second season of the Negro Industrial Baseball League, with teams representing Westinghouse Electric, Jones & Laughlin Steel, Duquesne Steel and the Alpha Club of Carnegie, Pa. The national black newspaper also noted that Carnegie Steel's black teams had dropped out of the league to compete against white steelworkers.

Two years later, 12-year-old Josh Gibson joined his father, a steelworker from Buena Vista, Georgia, and the rest of his family in a small house on Pittsburgh's North Side. Tall and muscular, Gibson quit school after ninth grade to work and play ball for Westinghouse Airbrake and Gimbel Bros. department stores. He was a third baseman with an average glove and powerful bat when Harold "Hooks" Tinker lured him to the Crawford Colored Giants, a popular sandlot team in the Hill District.

Who were Gibson's heroes? Not Lloyd and Paul Waner, Pie Traynor or Kiki Cuyler of the Pittsburgh Pirates. He admired Smokey Joe Williams, John Beckwith and Vic Harris, all members of the Homestead Grays, an independent black team whose early players worked at the huge Carnegie Steel mill on the other side of the Monongahela River.

By September 1930, the 19-year-old was catching Smokey Joe's fastball and hitting 450-foot home runs for the Grays at Forbes Field, Yankee Stadium and parks all over Western Pennsylvania, Eastern Ohio and Western New York. In 1931, his 40 homers led the team, which finished with a record of 143–29–2 against Negro National League teams and white semi-pro squads scattered throughout the East Coast and Midwest.

Grays owner Cumberland Posey, who had joined the Grays as a player in 1911, boasted of his team's dominance in "Posey's Points," a sports column in the *Courier*. But workers idled by the Depression often couldn't spare 25 or 50 cents to see the Grays play. Posey had trouble making payroll and in 1932 he lost Gibson and several other stars to the new Pittsburgh Crawfords, a club owned by numbers banker Gus Greenlee.

* * *

At 6'3"and 210 pounds, the man known as "Big Red" for his reddish hair was built for football but loved all sports, especially boxing. His stable of fighters included John Henry Lewis, a light heavyweight world champion. But Greenlee was much more than a sportsman. In an era when banks didn't loan to blacks, he was a loan officer, benefactor and political power broker in Pittsburgh's black neighborhoods. He always paid off his hits and local policemen for tips on numbers raids. He donated generously to churches and charities. Among the students he supported were his three brothers—two doctors and a lawyer.

"He created a city within the city, and he was the king," said Charles Harris, 89, of Silver Spring, Maryland, whose uncle was Greenlee's partner, Woogie Harris, and father was Charles "Teenie" Harris, chief photographer for the *Pittsburgh Courier*.

"They didn't just take, they gave back," Errol "Mobutu" Reynolds, 71, of the Hill District, said of Greenlee, Harris and Joe Robinson, another numbers banker who eventually took over the Crawford Grill. "They would take care of their own."

In a September 1930 article in the *Pittsburgh Post-Gazette*, Greenlee and Harris were described as the fathers of Pittsburgh's numbers racket. At 10 a.m., reporters described Hill District streets filled with runners openly carrying satchels of coins and escorted by armed men. "Negresses" with adding machines and piles of betting slips worked in the back rooms of buildings the newspaper called "Numbers Racket Nests."

One of them was Greenlee's club on Wylie Avenue, which was both his numbers headquarters and the city's hottest nightspot. In a silk suit with a Cuban cigar, Greenlee sat at the bar most evenings, surrounded by black and white politicians, athletes like novice football owner Art Rooney and entertainers Duke Ellington, Cab Calloway and other veterans of the Chitlin' Circuit. (Pittsburgh was their main stop between New York City and Chicago.)

At the bar one day, several Crawford Giants approached Greenlee and asked him to take over their sandlot team. He said yes, offering to put them on salary.

"We never thought of no salary," said Bill Harris, a team co-founder and brother of the Grays' Vic Harris. "We just wanted to play ball."

The numbers man went all in, raiding other teams for their best players and insisting that Tinker, Bill Harris and other veterans quit their day jobs and become pro ballplayers—or move along.

His biggest prize in 1931 was Satchel Paige, a tall Alabaman who came over from the Cleveland Cubs. Pitching relief in nearby McKeesport, Paige shut down the Grays and helped the Crawfords beat their crosstown rivals for the first time, 10–7.

* * *

A baseball team was a good way to launder numbers cash, but a bad investment. Passing the hat through a crowd of 6,000 fans on Decoration Day (Memorial Day) in 1931 brought in only $80. Greenlee's runners collected more than that daily on streets in the Hill District.

Greenlee continued his player raids in 1932. As the only black team owner to pay salaries instead of shares, he landed Josh Gibson, Oscar Charleston, Judy Johnson, Cool Papa Bell and Jud Wilson, all future Hall of Famers.

Greenlee also found a way around the white booking agents who controlled most of the Major League ballparks rented by Negro league teams. He built his own park, Greenlee Field, in the center of the Hill District. He partnered with two white men and paid half of the $100,000 cost himself. The field's 7,500 seats were slightly more than half-full on opening day, April 29, 1932, as the New York Black Yankees' Jesse Hubbard outdueled Paige for a 1–0 victory. The Crawfords finished with a 97–36 record and a loss of $15,000.

In 1933, a year before the first Major League All-Star Game, Greenlee came up with the East-West Game to showcase black baseball's best (and net him 10 percent of the profits). He also reorganized the Negro National League with teams mostly owned by gamblers and numbers bankers like him, including Robert Cole (Chicago American Giants), James Semler (New York Black

Yankees), Abe Manley (Newark Eagles), Alex Pompez (New York Cubans), Ed Bolden (Philadelphia Stars) and Tom Wilson (Baltimore Elite Giants).

Only the Chicago American Giants were a match for the Crawfords. Chicago edged them by one game in the first half standings of the 1933 season and the second half schedule wasn't finished. Greenlee, as league president, declared the Crawfords champions over the Giants' protests. Nobody challenged Pittsburgh in 1935 and '36, when the Crawfords won back-to-back NNL pennants.

Both gregarious and intimidating, Greenlee had no bodyguards and was rumored to have sent two protection racketeers to the bottom of one of the city's three rivers for harassing local shop owners. Yet he was also a notorious soft touch who would peel a $100 bill from a wad in his pocket for a worthy cause. When Paige married Janet Howard, a 21-year-old waitress from the Crawford Grill, Greenlee locked its doors and threw a big party.

His players admired his toughness. During an exhibition game between the Crawfords and a white barnstorming team led by Dizzy Dean, a fight between the catchers, Josh Gibson and Major Leaguer George Susce, turned into a melee. Greenlee's friend Art Rooney interceded with a judge to keep everyone out of jail.

Greenlee was often hauled into court but was never convicted. He posted bond, paid a $100 fine and went about his business. Losing the day's take was the much bigger hit.

"Numbers Baron Held for Court" blared a headline in the *Pittsburgh Press* on March 5, 1934. "16 Others Arrested in Hill District Raid." Greenlee's worst offense seemed to be the six slot machines found in the basement of the Belmont Hotel. He said they weren't his, that they had been left by someone named "Frank Steel," one of the phoniest names one could conjure in a steel town.

Another name in the article, one of the 16 others arrested, is much more authentic. Rufus Jackson of Homestead was the numbers man enlisted by Grays owner Cum Posey when he became fed up over losing players—and games—to Greenlee.

Though not as flashy as Big Red, Sonnyman Jackson was equally powerful in Homestead, a working class town of about 20,000 that boasted the world's largest steel mill during World War II. Jackson worked in a steel mill and had other jobs after leaving Georgia for Homestead in 1921. Eventually he built a business supplying hundreds of Seeburg and Wurlitzer jukeboxes to bars and restaurants in the Pittsburgh area. But his main sources of income were the Mon Valley's numbers racket and a string of gambling houses, with profits laundered through his Skyrocket Cafe.

Jackson had his own brushes with police and the underworld. In April 1935, when two blackmailers demanded $500, he agreed to a 2 a.m. meeting in an abandoned shack beneath a bridge linking Pittsburgh and Homestead. He tipped off the FBI, leading to a gunfight beneath the span that was renamed the Homestead Grays Bridge in 2002.

Once Jackson began bankrolling the Grays, the team never missed a payroll, said Buck Leonard, a future Hall of Fame first baseman who joined the Grays in 1934. Jackson, who bought the team a bus to match the one Greenlee got for the Crawfords in 1932, didn't know much about baseball at first.

"He got interested when he started riding the bus with us and heard how we talked and the lies we told," Leonard said.

* * *

The Grays joined the reborn Negro National League but were soon kicked out for raiding other teams' players, just as Greenlee had done to Posey in 1931–32. While Posey and Jackson began to rebuild the Grays, Greenlee's luck was running out amid a changing political climate. His Republican friends lost the mayor's seat to a Democratic reformer named William McNair and police raids became more frequent, and costly.

Speedy outfielder Cool Papa Bell remembered begging Greenlee not to kill a young man who had tipped off police about when the daily numbers take was counted. "I'm not going to have a boy killed," Greenlee told the ballplayer and put the young man on the next train out of town.

Reeling from a big numbers hit in 1936, Greenlee traded Gibson to the Grays for two players and $2,500 in cash. Charles Harris said Greenlee was in England for a John Henry Lewis fight when a hunch number—a favorite number that many people play every day—hit big in Pittsburgh. His uncle, Woogie Harris, was told to go to a certain room in Downtown Pittsburgh's Jenkins Arcade and see an Italian man. Woogie returned with $25,000 in cash, enough to pay off all the winners.

Another hit cost the partners $90,000, according to *Post-Gazette* reporter Ray Sprigle, who did a series on the numbers racket in February 1936. Despite the hits and police raids, Greenlee and Harris cemented a reputation for always paying off. According to Sprigle, bettors had one question for numbers runners: "Are you writing for the colored pool? They tell me that's the only honest pool."

Allan "Goody" Goode of Beltzhoover, the brother of TV newsman Malvin "Mal" Goode, was a runner for Greenlee and Harris, according to Bob Goode, his nephew. Though he also worked as a salesman and ran a bar, numbers provided his steadiest income. He was never caught with betting slips. "His memory was so good, he wouldn't write the numbers down. But he knew who won and who didn't."

In early 1937, Greenlee lost Paige and half of his starting nine to a

Dominican Republic dictator who relied on his country's love of baseball to retain power. In 1938, Greenlee sold the Crawfords and tore down Greenlee Field to make way for Bedford Dwellings, a public housing project.

Jackson and Posey, meanwhile, rebuilt the Grays with numbers money. The "Thunder Twins," Gibson and Leonard, led the team to nine straight pennants, from 1937–45, and the team won one more in '48. Despite that success, the Grays lost $45,000 in 1947–48, Jackson said. He died in 1949, three years after Posey, and the Grays disbanded in 1951.

Greenlee tried to get back into baseball, creating the United States League in 1945 with Branch Rickey's support. It folded after just two seasons as Rickey and others cherry-picked its best players for the Majors. Greenlee was nearly broke when he died in 1952. His funeral drew hundreds of mourners, both black and white.

Black baseball was always a lousy bet, yet Gus Greenlee and Sonnyman Jackson doubled and tripled down to build winning teams. Charles Harris, the nephew of Greenlee's partner, said his father didn't allow him to go alone to Gus' Crawford Grill or Woogie's barbershop. But he could join the thousands who jammed Greenlee Field to watch the Crawfords and Grays play.

"Woogie and Gus looked out for people. I called them benevolent gamblers," he said.

A Little More with Every Pitch

Lawrence Lawson

Let's peek into a car. Windows are fogged, so we'll have to squint. Nothing obscene occurring—just conversation and laughter on a cold night. He asks her what she studied in undergrad, and she talks to him about linguistics and language and identity. When she asks him the same, he (mostly) delivers a sonnet from Shakespeare about love and loss and the closing season of one's life.

"To love that well which thou must leave ere long," he concludes, tracing a frowny face into the condensation on the passenger window.

She turns to him and says, "Are you leaving or are you flirting with me?"

"Flirting, clearly," he says, but his next words open a divide in their nascent relationship that, at times, will push them apart and, at other times, will draw them together: "It's an ode to love and lost love, so, to me, it's a sonnet about October. The end of the most important season of the year."

She smiles, quick to catch on. "A baseball fan, too? Our friends were right. This could work out."

"Indeed," he says. "Lifelong, and tortured, Giants fan."

Her smile dims. "Born in Poway, California. Padres fan checking in."

"Ah," he says. "You're the one."

She unlocks the doors. "Get out."

"But…"

"Now."

∗   ∗   ∗

The next day at work, she receives a message over Gmail chat. She sighs. Had she really given him her email address, too? And who chats over email? Why didn't he just text? *Wait … why do I care?* she thinks.

109

His avatar, a black hat with orange script, flashes in the corner. *Can we talk?* his message says. She goes back to entering figures into a database for her boss. A minute later, a new message pop ups. *Hello?*

She logs out of Gmail. She's on a deadline. Her supervisor needs the data delivered to the Alumni Office by four so that whoever can do whatever they do. Phone banking or cold calls or something. Her grad school—*and his too,* she thinks—is "dialing for dollars" this evening, hoping to raise enough money to fund some of the linguistic research that—

Her phone chimes. His name pops up on the LCD screen of her flip phone, and of course his name makes her think of Larry Bowa and his short stint as manager for her San Diego team. *Such an old person's* name, she thinks. Her hand flips the phone open and his text is an image, which downloads automatically.

It's the Swinging Friar followed by one word. *Truce?*

*   *   *

They meet at what would, over the years, become their favorite pizza spot. He buys their slices, throws in for a salad and grabs two forks. "Figured we could share this while we wait for the pizza," he says, sliding onto the bench across from her.

"Thanks," she says, staring at the arugula and chopped walnuts, "but I detest anything green."

He pops the lid off the plastic container holding the salad. "Thank God I'm not an A's fan then." She laughs, and he relaxes a little. "You know ... that apostrophe drives me nuts."

"Me too," she replies. "Like ... there are very specific rules for how apostrophes are used."

"Right? What are they trying to show? It's clearly not possessive. Do they think an apostrophe is used to show a plural noun?"

She slaps the table. "Along with half of America."

"The same half that roots for the Yankees," he says.

"Ouch," she replies.

"So ... where were you for the '98 Series?"

She pushes her napkin across the table with a fork. "I had just started college. I went to the rec room to watch the game and quickly found I was the only one in the whole dorm who cared. I was the pitcher for our softball team. You'd think a few of my teammates would have been interested. Nope. Watched every game by myself."

"Luckily there were only four," he says.

"Damn Yankees," they say in unison. She raises an eyebrow, and he smiles. The pizza comes, and the silence is filled with the scent of crispy pepperoni and thyme.

"So, your dad's a Padres fan too, I take it?" he asks between bites.

"Mom. Believe it or not, women can be the sports fans in the family. My dad follows the Padres, too, of course."

He puts up his hands in protest. "My mom was the sports fan in the house, too. Taught me to love baseball. Tried to teach me to love hockey. Less successful there."

"So why the Giants?"

"Geography … and sibling rivalry. My brother was a Dodgers fan."

Her face twists, and she makes a drama of swallowing her food. "You're related to a Dodgers fan?"

"I guess there are worse things than being a Giants fan, huh?"

"Even Joseph McCarthy wasn't a Dodgers fan. And that guy was evil."

They took their last bites of pizza. A TV blared in the background, Joe Buck's unmistakable voice running down the line-ups for the Boston Red Sox and St. Louis Cardinals. A busboy, decked out in clothing more appropriate for a boutique clothing store than a pizza place, grabs their plates and shuffles off toward the trash.

"So," he says.

"So," she replies.

"My friends are watching the game tonight. You're welcome to join."

"Giants fans, too?"

"We do live in Monterey. The likelihood is high, but I like to think of my group of friends as multi-denominational."

"Padres fans?"

"In that, you're like a unicorn. I should take photos of you and send them to National Geographic."

She grabs his hand. "Let's go."

*   *   *

Less than a year later, they're standing in front of 80 of their closest friends and family, hands clasped and rings secured. He works a line about baseball into his vow, and during the reception she tosses a softball tied to her bouquet. Their official honeymoon consists of a jaunt into the Santa Rosa backcountry to stay at a B&B nestled in a copse of oak trees clinging to the side of a mountain, but their "real," albeit unofficial, honeymoon takes them to Ukraine for what will be two years, two months, and 19 days of Peace Corps service. (They are both Peace Corps Masters International students, so Peace Corps service is strategically placed between two years of Master's Degree coursework in Teaching English to Speakers of Other Languages— TESOL for short.)

Serving abroad, they miss the 2005, 2006, and 2007 World Series, but they are not completely divorced from the sport they love. They follow their teams from afar but have little to cheer about. They fill the void by taking part in a summer camp devoted to teaching young women the sport of softball, a camp that is remarkable in a country where women are not often expected to be interested in sports. Along with the sport, these young women learn about leadership and belonging.

She teaches the young women how to wind up a pitch and throw a rise, a fastball, and a drop pitch. He plays catch at the margins of the gym where they are practicing and gets hit in the face twice with a ball because, instead of watching the balls being flung at his face, he's watching the muscle and the sinew of his wife's body. The curves and the explosive pop. He came into her life story too late to see her on the NCAA field, so what he is seeing is novel and heart stopping. He later describes her, in the journal he kept throughout Peace Corps, as *рідка енергія*, or liquid energy. Every motion of her body implies that she was, in fact, born for this movement—the grip, the push-off, the stride, the release. And he can't stop watching.

That is, until he catches a thrown ball to the cheek.

*   *   *

In 2006, the San Diego Padres CEO, Sandy Alderson, decides he wants a new look for manager, so he allows Bruce Bochy, then manager for the San Diego Padres, to interview with the San Francisco Giants.

On October 27, 2006, Bruce Bochy becomes the new manager of the San Francisco Giants.

In Ukraine, they register this news, but life consumes them, and they let the news fall to the back burner.

*   *   *

Back in the United States at the end of 2007, they return to grad school (graduating in December 2008), and he lands his dream job in, of all places, San Diego. For a number of reasons, she's thrilled to be in San Diego, and somewhere in the top five is the fact that she can see her San Diego Padres in person. Soon after the 2009 season starts, they get tickets for a game, Padres vs. Giants, and he soon discovers the reason for her Giants hatred.

Petco Park, home to the San Diego Padres, is filled, from field to upper deck, with orange and black. When the Giants score, the stadium erupts with cheers. When the Padres score, and eventually beat the Giants, the stadium murmurs with the shouts of a sprinkling of Padres fans.

"Now you know why I dislike Giants fans. More of them here than Padres fans," she says. "We're a city of transplants, and all of them seem to be baseball fans."

*   *   *

Much to her chagrin, 2010 happens.

Having lived in San Diego for nearly two years, she is slowly converting her husband into a Padres fan—or, at least, a less obnoxious Giants fan. But the season, for both teams, comes down to October 3, 2010. Venue: AT&T Park. The Giants have entered the three-game series needing to win just one game against the Padres to clinch the NL West.

But they lose to the Padres on October 1. And October 2.

Her heart is full. The Padres might win the NL West.

His heart is full of dread. The Giants might lose the NL West.

The whole series, and season, for both teams, comes down to one, cool San Francisco evening, and the otherwise happily married couple listens to the final three outs sitting in their car, in the garage, battling static and the ionosphere. When reliever Brian Wilson raises his arms in victory, she reaches over and turns the radio off.

"I almost had you. You were almost a Padres fan," she says.

"No you didn't. I've been a Giants fan since I was nine years old," he says. "Not likely to change."

"I almost had you."

"Bruce Bochy is a damn good manager."

"Please … don't," she says.

For Christmas that year, she presents him with a gift. Inside, huddled within a distinct cardboard box, are eight DVDs chronicling the San Francisco Giants' path to the World Series Trophy.

I guess I love you this much, the note reads.

And he thinks back to the night she playfully kicked him out of her car.

*   *   *

Their love of the sport is shared by a number of their friends, and they decide to sign up for co-ed softball. Their first season ends in flames as the team's pitcher abandons the team for the final three games of the season. She's the natural choice to pitch given her NCAA resume, but she demurs. "These guys are trying to tear the face off the ball, and there's no chance I'm going to stand in front of them while they do it," she says. So, between the day they find out they'd been abandoned by their pitcher and the date of their next game, she teaches him how to pitch a ball, how to field his position, and how to battle through a tough game.

And, the next Sunday, he takes the mound.

They lose 16–3.

It's slow-pitch softball, so the mechanics are different, but she takes him out to the field again and teaches him what she knows. He's reminded of Ukraine and the young women she taught and the *рідка енергія*. Despite having been married for six years, he finds himself falling in love a little more with every pitch.

The next game they lose 11–6.

"Progress," she says.

She teaches him how to step into his pitch, how to transfer energy from his stride into his release. The ball lands on the plate more often than not but not often enough to allow him to stop beating himself up. She touches him, lightly, on the shoulder and says, "You're getting better. Be nice to yourself."

The last game of the season, they lose. 9–8.

* * *

Their lives expand as lives do. New friends, more teaching, more grading, more softball, more projects, more responsibilities. All the while, he's working his dream job in San Diego while she's looking for hers.

Then, eventually, she finds it.

In the winter of 2012, she interviews for a full-time professorship in Los Angeles, and she gets the job. The discussion is brief.

This is your career.

If we could handle Ukraine, we can do anything.

Take it.

I'm taking it.

And he helps her pack, find an apartment, and move to Los Angeles. He remains in San Diego, nearby his wife's hometown team, while she starts a new and distant life within the shadow of Dodger Stadium. He takes the train north on weekends, or she drives down to visit him and her family. Friday through Sunday, they hug and laugh and touch. Monday through Thursday, what they have is the telephone and Skype and Facetime.

And baseball.

* * *

In 2013, she takes him to his first game at Dodger Stadium. They're playing the Cardinals, another team they both dislike together, so they feel fine rooting (ever so slightly) for the home team. Slowly, through several innings, they begin to relax. Dodger fans aren't so bad. In fact, they're sort of nice. One even offered to buy him a Dodger Dog because he'd never had one.

"At least," she points out, "they're paying attention to the game. They know when to cheer without being told by the scoreboard." Not her experience, clearly, in San Diego.

The season he takes in his first game at Dodger Stadium, the Dodgers cruise to an NL West Championship while the Giants and the Padres tie for third place, both teams finishing 16 games back. There's a lot to commiserate about, but she won't put up with his dourness. "They won the World Series in 2010 and 2012. You have absolutely *zero* to complain about."

"But they tied with the *Padres,*" he whines.

And she points to the front door of her apartment. "Get out."

"But…"

"Now."

*   *   *

Then 2014 happens, and he adds to his collection of DVDs.

She says, "This is the last time I'm buying a boxed-set of Giants DVDs for you for Christmas."

*   *   *

Winter 2015 arrives, and she's applying for a new job in San Diego. It's nearly as good as the one she has in Los Angeles but "it's in San Diego," she says. Full-time jobs are scarce in their field, and she's doubtful. Undeterred, he preps her for the interview—hours and hours of possible questions, critical feedback, tears, and second tries. In the end, she kills the first round and gets a final interview.

"I could come back to San Diego," she says over the phone. "We could live together again."

"Just in time to watch San Francisco win it all again in 2016."

"Good point. I'll call HR in the morning and rescind my acceptance."

"I'll be shutting up now," he replies.

Ten days after the final interview, she still hasn't heard from HR regarding a job offer. She's down. Usually, HR calls within a few days to offer a job. They take their time when they're calling with a rejection. They both need a pick-me-up, so he goes to the store and buys something he hopes will help. For several weeks, they've seen a pile of stuffed turtles, dressed only in a holiday beanie, perched tantalizingly close to the checkout stand. Every time they pass through with their groceries, she says," Oh … look how cute he is!" When he offers to buy one of the little guys for her, she replies, "We don't need stuff."

However, he feels differently.

The turtle sits on his lap as he takes the train north from Oceanside to Glendale. He strokes its shell, trying to extract some sort of luck or hope or something from its polyester shell. *Help her come home,* he thinks.

When she picks him up from the train station, he presents her with the turtle and says, "It's a good luck charm."

She hugs it to her chest. "You shouldn't have." Then she holds it aloft and asks, "Are you going to bring me this job?"

"That's the idea," he says. "I thought you needed something to lift your spirits."

She kisses the turtle and asks, "What shall we name you?"

"How about Job? Or Please-Offer-Me-The-Job? Or I-Deserve-This-Job?" he says.

She smiles. "Job isn't a name."

"You clearly haven't read the Bible."

"Different pronunciation. How about Jobby, then?"

"Like the house elf?"

"The what?"

"Never mind. I like the name. How would you spell it?"

"J-A-B-I."

"Okay," he says. "But if you don't get the job and move back home, we're going to have to change its name."

"Agreed," she replies.

Three days later, she calls, crying. "We can still call him Jabi."

*   *   *

In October of 2016, the happy couple lives together, once again, in San Diego. The Padres have a ho-hum season, once again. The Giants have a thrilling, but this time uneventful, even-year playoff run. However, there are more pressing things on their minds.

"What does it say?" she asks.

"Congratulations?"

"What?"

"Congratulations," he replies. "You're going to be a mom."

"No, really," she says. "What does it say?"

"Two lines. We're pregnant."

"No."

"Yes."

"Yes."

"Yes."

*   *   *

Weeks later, after he's read *What to Expect When You're Expecting* and *From the Hips*, he brings to her the most pressing question that the books have been unable to answer. "Do we raise our child as a Giants fan or a Padres fan?"

"It doesn't matter."

"But..."

"It. Doesn't. Matter." She hugs him close. "However," she adds, "I already bought a Padres onesie."

My Inheritance

KAREN HAMILTON

My grandpa chuckled every time he saw the big basket on my softball glove. I didn't really understand why my glove was so funny to him until I saw his 1940s baseball mitt, barely larger than his hand and well worn in the palm. "You actually had to know how to catch," he used to say. My grandpa never cared much for the showy basket catches of modern day outfielders. He also wasn't sentimental about material possessions. As he aged, he got rid of a lot of old keepsakes that he didn't have any use for. When we didn't see his glove around, we feared it had been tossed.

I inherited my love of baseball from my mom, who inherited hers from her daddy. In my house, it was my mom who counted down the days until spring training and always informed me when it was time for pitchers and catchers to report. The subscription to Sports Illustrated on the coffee tables was hers. To this day, she's the one who keeps me informed of new rules or big trades.

My mom grew up in Riverside, California, a Dodger and later Angels, fan. She was a Junior Angel, now called the Junior Angels Kids Club, in the early 1960s. "I remember the drive into LA in the station wagon. If traffic was light and we had some time we would stop at Clifton's Cafeteria in West Covina for a piece of pie before the game." She doesn't think there was a similar kids club for the Dodgers, but she does remember some kind of promotion with Fritos that they would use for a coupon.

While she doesn't remember many individual Angels' players, other than Jim Fregosi, she remembers all the Dodgers. There wasn't much turnover between 1960 and 1965 when she was an avid pre-teen fan. Maury Wills was one of her favorites, but she can name a dozen others: Koufax, Drysdale, Roseboro, Hodges, Gilliam, Moon, Willie Davis, Tommy Davis, then later Frank Howard, and into 1970s, Garvey, Russell, Lopes and Cey. And that was just off the top of her head. Her memories of early Dodgers games were watching people in the stands keep score and that "everyone had their transistor radios and listened to Vin Scully." She also remembers that her parents "had a mattress in the back of the station wagon and a lot of times I'd be asleep before we got out of the parking lot. I remember being carried in to bed when I was little, but then I got too big and had to wake up to walk to bed."

*   *   *

Growing up in San Diego, I was, and still am, a Padres fan. Though there was no station wagon or pie involved in my early baseball memories, there were fireworks and the San Diego Chicken. I was too young to remember much about the 1984 World Series team, but I cherished my Mother's Cookies baseball card giveaway with those players. Those were the years of brown and gold, and later brown and orange, uniforms. I remember Steve Garvey, Goose Gossage, Carmelo Martinez, Tim Flannery, and Garry Templeton. And from the time I was two years old until I was almost finished with college, I had the privilege of watching #19 play outfield for the Padres.

Tony Gwynn's numbers speak for themselves: eight time batting champ, a .338 lifetime batting average, 3,141 career hits, five gold gloves, and named to the All-Star team 15 times. You could always count on Tony to find a hole, especially the 5.5 hole between shortstop and third base. They said he could see the fielders move as the pitch was coming and hit it where they weren't, like if a second baseman was cheating to cover the base on the steal, he could adjust while the pitch was on its way and hit it behind the second baseman. He was known to be serious student of the game, watching countless hours of video of his swing or of opposing pitchers, before that kind of preparation was common practice.

I went to school with Tony Gwynn's kids and my mom would see him around town, often picking up clothes from the dry cleaners. He had a high-pitched voice that didn't seem to fit his body and the most infectious laugh. He was a humble superstar, so generous with fans. And he stayed. Tony Gwynn could have gone to a better team for more money, but he remained Mr. Padre. He was proud to have spent his whole career in San Diego, and that kind of devotion is increasingly rare in baseball.

*   *   *

My early love for baseball translated into a love for softball. I began playing on recreational teams when I was seven years old and continued to play competitively through college. The early team names depended on our randomly assigned color: when we were royal blue, we named ourselves the "501 Blues." When we were maroon, we became "Raspberry Ice." I began as a shortstop, modeling myself after the consistent fielding of Garry Templeton. In those early years, it was often difficult for girls to throw strikes, so I began to pitch. I never threw hard, but I had control. I was known for my excellent drop ball and a deceptive changeup.

I pitched all throughout high school and college. My dad would catch for me in the backyard. We would blast Jimi Hendrix or George Thorogood or Genesis from inside the house. The backyard wasn't quite long enough, so I'd pitch at a diagonal. My dad even rigged up an outdoor light so I could pitch after dark. We must have spent hours per week out there over several years. Yet my dad was never too tired to catch for me, despite long hours of running his own business. He'd put his hat on backward and half-squat, thanks to bad knees from years of wrestling. We'd go through simulated batters and keep the count on them. I always had to throw a good strike as the final pitch before heading indoors.

As my teams grew more competitive, our names grew more serious. My travel ball teams were the "Scorpions," and the "Cobras." The Cobras were a travel ball team I played on from the time I was in sixth grade through early high school. Most of the girls on the team were older than me and had been playing together for a long time. As an only child, I am grateful to this team for giving me the opportunity to have sisters. These were sisters in the sense that they weren't necessarily the girls I would have chosen for friends. Many were bratty or boy crazy, perpetually running late because they were worried about the bows in their hair. Their dads were too intense, and often served as assistant coaches who were either way too hard on or unrealistically enamored of their daughters. I didn't always get along or have much in common with the vast majority of these sisters, but there was a handful with whom I did.

I met my friend Michelle on the Cobras. She was a year older, and we went to different middle schools, so we always spent those first few minutes of practice catching up on the week's news while we ran our laps. She was the team's main pitcher and I was her backup. She was always a lot better but I really didn't mind. We were fast friends. In retrospect, this was likely due to the fact that neither of us really fit in with the rest of our teammates. We didn't have the coolest clothes, didn't hang in the popular circles at school, and were less concerned with what people thought of us. Michelle and I would spend hours in her room making up silly songs or writing creative stories. She got a full-ride scholarship to play softball in college, while I walked on at a Division III school. She set all kinds of records with her pitching. The only award my team ever got was for our GPA.

Michelle is the only softball friend from middle or high school I have kept in touch with. I don't know that I would have stuck with the game if it weren't for her friendship. She made me look forward to going to practices and those long weekends away at tournaments. We were in each other's weddings and, despite living on different coasts, have stayed close as adults.

*   *   *

I was working part-time teaching ESL at the local community college when I received an email from a former professor from graduate school. She had been approached by a company that teaches English to professional athletes asking if she knew of any ESL instructors who also had an interest in baseball. Naturally, I came to mind so she put us in touch. I couldn't believe I was being offering the possibility of combining my two passions: ESL and baseball! I was uniquely qualified for the position because of my ESL training and my familiarity with baseball vocabulary, especially the language of pitching mechanics. The position was with the High A team in the LA Dodgers' organization: the Rancho Cucamonga Quakes. Though their field was a two-hour drive from my home in San Diego, I accepted the position. My task was teaching the players a range of topics, from communicating with their host families to understanding the coaches' instructions to explaining an injury to the team trainer.

I quickly got to work preparing myself for my dream job. I began following the team closely, printing out lineups and game summaries from their games and accessing player statistics online. I bought several baseball magazines from the bookstore and cut out images of players in action so that they could describe the actions. I bought a hand-held white board and laminated a cut out of a baseball field. On my first day, my supervisor directed me to a box suite directly behind home plate. It was a home game that evening, so the grounds crew was diligently preparing the field. The stadium was empty but the music was blasting while they worked. Not a bad view from my new office, I thought.

My students were three Spanish-speaking players, two from the Dominican Republic and one from Puerto Rico. They came to my makeshift classroom in workout clothes, groggy as if they had just woken up (I had yet to realize how nocturnal the lifestyle of minor league baseball was). They didn't have pencils or notebooks and I quickly got the impression that they didn't particularly want to be there. We covered some basics, names, positions, and favorite players. The two guys from the Dominican Republic admired Albert Pujols. One of them proudly explained that he was from the same hometown as Pujols.

After about 20 minutes, they were ready to leave. They were hungry and needed to get dressed and report to the field in about an hour. I made them stay almost the full 90 minutes, but tried to distract them with short, interactive activities. We looked at their stats and they joked with each other in Spanish about having a bad night or sitting on the bench. They learned action verbs like run, steal, slide, catch, and throw. Then they learned the past tense of those verbs. We played charades so they could practice the action words.

I showed them videos of the big league Dodgers and had them describe what was happening. They were good sports, but it was obvious that a coach or player development manager was requiring them to attend my classes.

As a fan at minor league games, I always admired how hard the players worked and how it seemed they really had a love for the game. Unlike in the Majors, where players occasionally don't hustle or are afraid of getting hurt, these guys seemed to truly love the game and wanted to prove themselves. Little did I realize how cutthroat the Minor Leagues were. If your buddy makes it to the big leagues, that's one fewer spot for you. So while they were happy for each other and tried to be supportive, you could see in their faces that they were petrified of not making it. Most of them had been playing baseball full time since they were young boys and had nothing to fall back on if they didn't make it.

Minor League players make very low salaries, but from what I could gather, they sent most of their money back home to their families. The students in my class lived with a host family. Four of them shared one bedroom. They cooked chicken and rice daily and pitched in to buy a used car that they shared. They told me about the poverty of their hometowns and the pressure to be successful here. I thought about how one year's minimum salary in the Major Leagues ($507,500) would compare to what their families earned back at home and what they currently made.

Eventually, I got a full-time ESL job that didn't allow me to teach at Rancho Cucamonga during the summers any more, but I continued to follow my former students' careers. A couple of them toiled at the single A level and then returned home. A few moved up to double A and then triple A. I had never expected that one of my handful of students would make it to the Major Leagues, but so far, three of them have played with the Dodgers (however briefly). One of them even made this year's playoff roster as a reliever.

I took pictures of the television during his major league debut. He came into the game with one on and one out. Would you believe he faced his idol, Albert Pujols, and got him to ground into a double play? Each time I watch him run in from the bullpen and take the mound, I think how the nervousness I feel must only be a fraction of what my parents felt all those years watching me during softball. This wasn't my child; he was my student for one brief summer. But I wanted so badly for him to succeed and really make it in the big leagues. I wanted his years of childhood dedication to pay off, for his sacrifices to be worth it. During his pitching coach's visit to the mound I tried to read their lips to see if his English had improved. The catcher wasn't out there translating, so at least they were communicating, I thought.

*   *   *

This past summer, my husband, parents, and I visited the Baseball Hall of Fame in Cooperstown. Michelle was getting married in upstate New York and it was the perfect occasion for a family trip. We spent a couple days taking in the plaques and the history. And while I appreciated seeing the old jerseys, scuffed bases, dirty uniforms, and scorecards, I realized that for me, baseball is so much more than the memorabilia. It's my mom's stories about time with her family as a child, or my own memory of a lasting childhood friendship. It's my grandpa's hitting advice or my dad catching me in the backyard. It's the challenging world of the minor leagues, soothed by the success of a former student who made it. It's all of these sweet moments put together, like a slice of pie on the way to a Dodgers game, which I cherish and will pass on along with my grandpa's glove.

Citizen Cal

Robyn Barberry

I spent my entire childhood watching Cal Ripken, Jr., play baseball. From the comfort of my parents' arms as a newborn during the 1983 World Series until his retirement during my freshman year at Towson University (a few weeks after 9/11), Cal spent his entire career with the Baltimore Orioles and played a record 2,632 consecutive games. I was raised outside of Baltimore in a family of baseball super-fans, the kind who'd watch every televised game on a hazy tube TV on hot nights, then spend breakfast checking box scores and reading Kevin Cowherd's analysis of the game in the *Baltimore Sun*. My dad collects everything that ever had anything to do with the Orioles: photos, baseball cards, posters, game balls, anything with an autograph on it or a story behind it. When he could, he'd take us to the games and explain everything baseball to us. I can remember being three or four and falling asleep on the metal bleachers at Memorial Stadium only to be awakened by the heavy vibrations of 50,000 O's fans cheering somebody home. It was probably Cal. He was bigger than Michael Jackson in Baltimore.

Dads like mine loved Cal because they never ran out of fodder for sports talk with other O's fans. Cal was a rock star on both sides of the ball; easily the best shortstop since Honus Wagner. Moms loved Cal's dreamy ice blue eyes and the way his white, black and orange uniform accentuated his assets. And of course, he was a squeaky-clean role model for the kids. Cal demonstrated good sportsmanship on the field and the manners of a gentleman everywhere else. He always found a way to give back to the community. Moms were especially excited when Cal became a spokesman (spokes model?) for the Dairy Counsel. Just about every kid I knew had a life-sized poster in his bedroom of Cal holding a carton of milk, which read, "Drink your milk and see how you measure up to Cal Ripken, Jr." Those who weren't lactose intolerant obeyed, although most of us failed to attain his 6'4" stature. Kids fought over who got to wear the number 8 on the back of their rec league uniforms.

Shortstop was the only position that mattered (even more than pitcher). When we wanted to take a sick day from school, our parents would remind us that Cal showed up every day. Above all things, Cal was a Harford County kid like me, my brother, and the dozens of kids who ran our neighborhood ragged all summer long.

When Cal was inducted in the Major League Baseball Hall of Fame in 2007, droves of Orioles fans made a pilgrimage to Cooperstown to see our native son permanently emblazoned onto baseball history. My entire family went except for me. I had just gotten married and was settling into my new home in Aberdeen, which is also Cal's hometown.

On the surface, Aberdeen isn't much. It's a Maryland suburb halfway between Baltimore and Wilmington, exit 85 on I-95, dotted with convenience stores, fast food restaurants, liquor stores, drug treatment centers, and funeral homes, as well as a bowling alley, a renowned Italian restaurant called the Olive Tree, a smattering of hotels, a fine jewelry store called Saxons Diamonds, and churches of nearly every Christian denomination. The schools are good, but not great (6/10 on greatschools.net). Most of the neighborhoods are modest gatherings of ranches, cottages, colonials, and cape cods. You'll also find gorgeous Victorian painted ladies standing tall in vast lots, while houses the size of RVs cower behind them. Downtown Aberdeen boasts a red brick post office, police station and firehouse. The library was built at the height of ugly 20th century architecture, but its frills are its literature, a rotating display of art from local students, and the nicest librarians in Harford County. (There's also a baseball diamond embedded into the carpet in the children's section.)

At the center of everything is a big park with a playground and a bandstand. You're just as likely to spot a struggling addict in those places as you are a stereotypical suburban stroller-pushing mom like me or a couple of kids throwing grounders and pop-ups. Aberdeen was supposed to be the place where we made our starter home, not where we were going to start a family. But Cal Ripken, Jr., grew up here. And he turned out all right.

Like all legends, Cal Ripken, Jr., had to start somewhere. His story started in Aberdeen on August 24, 1960, when Cal was born to Cal Ripken, Sr. (affectionately known as Rip) and his lovely wife and high school sweetheart, Vi. Mr. and Mrs. Ripken both had lived in Aberdeen all their lives and wanted to raise their children there. Rip loved baseball from an early age, probably because the sport had been prominent in Aberdeen culture since its inception. When he played as a catcher for Aberdeen High School, the Eagles won three county championships and celebrated an undefeated season in 1952. Post high school, Rip was drafted by the Baltimore Orioles farm system and found himself playing all across the country from Arizona to Florida to the Midwest and the Northeast and finally back in Aberdeen for two games with the Pheasants. As a baseball enthusiast herself and Rip's number one fan, Vi was an ardent supporter of his chosen career and sometimes found herself taking on the role of scorekeeper. In an interview, Rip said some of the amateur players were even better than the pros and that people came from all around to watch them play. Vi chimed in, "Nobody could afford boats or whatever and that's where they went." After seven years of repetitive motion, his arm and shoulder hinted that it was time to shift over to the other side of the game. So, Rip hung up his catcher's gear and grabbed a clipboard to coach in the minors.

By this point, Rip and Vi had expanded their team at home. Though Rip treated all of his players like sons, being a father to his own children was challenging because he was frequently on the road, while Vi held down the fort in their modest Aberdeen home. Vi was the one shouting Cal's name from the sidelines of his little league and high school games. She probably knew the game better than any of the other team moms. But when Cal Sr. was home, he always took time to teach his children the ins and outs of baseball and how to show people respect on and off the field. When Cal was a teenager, Rip had finally moved up in the coaching world and was managing for the Baltimore Orioles. He was delighted to be back in Aberdeen with Vi and the kids and made up for lost time by inviting Cal and his younger brother Billy to Memorial Stadium to practice.

It paid off in 1978, when Cal Ripken, Jr., graduated from Aberdeen High School. It's the same school his parents graduated from; the same school my kids will attend. There are beautiful portraits of Rip and Cal and other famous Aberdonians hanging in the sunny hallway that greets you when you enter the school as if to say, "You can make it here." Before he even finished high school Cal had a spot lined up on a Baltimore Orioles minor league team and a Maryland State Championship under his belt. I had the good fortune of visiting the Aberdeen Archives and seeing Cal's high school yearbooks. He was a shoo-in for the varsity team his freshman year. The pictures of him in the baseball spreads revealed a confident player with sophisticated posture and profound intensity in his crystal blue eyes. His dark shaggy hair came to his ears; a far cry from the buzz cut he wore in my childhood or the "Mr. Clean" look he dons these days. In August of 1981, Cal started his career with the Baltimore Orioles. A year later, he was named Rookie of the Year. In 1983, the Orioles won the World Series and Cal earned the MVP. A few years later, in 1991, Cal proved he wasn't just an incredible shortstop with his .323 batting average, 34 home runs, 114 RBI, 5 triples, 46 doubles, 6 stolen bases, and his lowest strikeout rate ever. P.S. Guess who won the Home Run Derby?

On September 6, 1995, in what was considered to be the most memorable moment of his career, Cal broke Lou Gehrig's consecutive game streak record when he showed up ready to play his 2,131st game. Despite the seemingly endless standing ovation, the victory lap around the vast park, and all the ensuing fanfare, Cal presented himself as a very humble man. He said, "As I grew up here, I not only had dreams of being a big league ballplayer, but also of being a Baltimore Oriole." That night, he was handed a $75,000 check to build a "Field of Dreams." He would later use it to build Ripken Stadium back home in Aberdeen and start the Ripken Baseball enterprise with his brother, Billy, who also played for the Orioles. Game 2,131 was the climax of Cal's career with the Orioles, but he continued to appear in 19 All-Star games. He also joined the 3,000 hit club, with a career total of 3,184 singles. He ended his streak at 2,362 on September 20, 1998. A member of the Ripken family told me that it was because Cal Sr., was rushed to the hospital with bronchitis and learned it was cancer. Just before the publication of his book "The Ripken Way," a guide to baseball and life, Cal Sr., passed on March 25, 1999. Cal Ripken, Jr., retired from professional baseball on October 6, 2001. In 2002, Cal brought a minor league baseball team from Utica, New York, to Aberdeen, Maryland, and changed their name to the "Ironbirds," a reference to the military planes from Aberdeen Proving Ground that circle the area. In this town of 15,000, where the collars are mostly blue, gray, and camo, the stadium and its facility give our community character. Everyone goes to an Ironbirds game hoping to catch a glimpse of Cal … or to witness the birth of the next Iron Man.

The Cal Ripken World Series is the pinnacle of the summer season at Ripken Stadium, and in Aberdeen. The annual event is usually held in August and brings in 10 top teams from the U.S., Maryland, including one from Harford County, and teams from eight countries around the world. A parade through my neighborhood celebrates the arrival of these pubescent boys who are demonstrating a knack for double plays and doubles. They've traveled a long way to show what they've got on the diamonds Cal built. Thousands of World Series visitors stay in Aberdeen hotels, including the Courtyard situated adjacent to the stadium, which resembles the famous warehouse wall that hovers over right field at Camden Yards. Some players stay with Aberdeen host families who love the experience of exchanging cultures and bonding over a love for baseball. Visitors dine in Aberdeen restaurants, including everything from the famed, locally owned Italian restaurant the Olive Tree to Panera and McDonald's franchises. It's not uncommon to see entire teams roaming Target for deodorant and Walgreen's for sunflower seeds and Double Bubble. The games are open to the public, as Ripken Stadium is owned by the City of Aberdeen.

Ripken Stadium's presence has helped to change the image of a place once perceived to be crime-ridden into an "All America City" where people like me live, work, and raise our families. My three boys are still very young, but my husband and I dream of having our sons participate in The Ripken

Experience—Aberdeen, Powered by Under Armour. Dozens of fields and practice facilities are available where young baseball players are coached and conditioned, play games and tournaments and get to experience on a small scale what it might feel like to be in the big leagues. Some fields have features of famous Major League stadiums, like a mini "Green Monster" in Fenway Park and a brick backstop at Wrigley Field. Cal and Billy have even dedicated a field to their dad to preserve his memory and make him a permanent part of the Aberdeen baseball legacy.

Cal's passion for youth sports education has expanded beyond the baseball field and found its way into bookstores across the country and on the Internet. Somehow Cal finds time to write books on mentoring and training for coaches and parents, as well as a series of short novels with Baltimore sportswriter Kevin Cowherd, called "Cal Ripken Jr.'s All-Stars" which are centered on various themes of character and good sportsmanship for young readers. It's Cal's way of inspiring the next generation without having to throw on a uniform. "Hothead," the first story, tells the story of a shortstop named Connor who needs to learn how to control his temper. They're the kind of books I would have read when I was 10. They're the kind of books I want to read to my own kids.

Fortunately, I married an Orioles fan who shares my passion for baseball. He won a Dizzy Dean World Series Championship when he was 12, and now he's starting to coach our oldest two sons in rec ball. Like my dad, he watches the O's with the boys, explains what a strike zone is and why a ball is foul or fair. The past few years have been favorable for the Orioles, but I don't feel the same raw excitement I did when I was a kid and Cal was still in the game. I encouraged my oldest son to choose a favorite player. He decided to go with center fielder and team clown, Adam Jones, who is from San Diego. We love watching him play, but I can't help but wonder, when his contract is up, is he going to want to stick around? Adam does some wonderful things for Baltimore, but there's no real reason to stay here. San Diego has some of the most beautiful beaches in America and nearly perfect weather to match. His family is there. Baltimore was always home for Cal, so he never left. His commitment to home is rare.

On September 20, 2016, I read in the *Baltimore Sun* that after 13 years, Cal was moving the Cal Ripken World Series out of Aberdeen and selling the Ironbirds. Many Aberdonians were upset. Even the mayor was blindsided. As for the team, I don't care who owns it, as long as they stay in town, the players show up, and everyone plays good ball. But, the Cal Ripken World Series means so much to a town so drab that its biggest excitement in the past few years was the grand opening of the Chick-fil-A. Many of us live and work in the same town. (I live and work on the same street.) It gets old. So when people from all around the world visit, it offers us the chance to discover a glimpse outside of our own. At the same time, it forces us to present the best versions of ourselves and of our town. It's an opportunity to showcase our greatest asset, Ripken baseball. And there are people all over the world who think it's worth coming to visit Aberdeen to experience it firsthand.

It costs Ripken's organization $100K to run the event, but it didn't seem like much money for someone who started off as a middle-class kid from Aberdeen and wound up becoming very wealthy. On September 21, 2016, his 12.5 million dollar, 6-bedroom, 10-bath home was listed. It is situated on a velvety green chunk of property on the other side of Baltimore. As I was scrolling through photo after photo of his palatial domicile, teeming with rich woods, jewel tones, baroque patterns, and overstuffed furniture with fringe, another news story informed me that Cal was selling his stakes in the Ironbirds. His spokesman, John Maroon, insisted that Cal's decisions to move the Cal Ripken World Series out of Aberdeen and sell his share of the Ironbirds had nothing to do with his divorce from his wife of nearly 30 years, Kelly. If it did, I would understand. It would offer me peace of mind to know that Cal's hands are tied and that if he could have it any other way, he would. So far, we haven't gotten any answers. Some longtime Ironbirds fans I spoke with said they heard that the Ironbirds had been losing money for a while. "We'd go to big games and entire sections would be empty," one fan said. Has Minor League baseball lost its thrill? Is the economy cutting into people's entertainment budgets? Or has the Cal factor fizzled out? One of the Ironbirds' fans says they used to see him at the stadium all the time, but now, he rarely makes an appearance. The hometown hero is missing.

At the Aberdeen Room and Archives, I received a rare gift—the chance to watch an interview with Rip and Vi from 1994. In the video, the interviewer asks Rip and Vi why they decided to stay in Aberdeen. Rip says, "I was born and raised here. You stay where you come from. It's only natural that you stay in this particular area. When you have roots here, you're gonna stay here." Vi's answer was simple, "I consider Aberdeen my home. It's been my family's home. The whole community is like a tiny little family. I just enjoy it." Rip and Vi were from a simpler time and they kept each other grounded in the community they'd called home since birth. Why go anywhere else? Everything they needed was in Aberdeen. Even though he was raised in Aberdeen, played baseball in Baltimore and lived for many years in the rural area just outside of the city, Cal has the means and, perhaps, the desire to pursue bigger and better things. Even though some Aberdonians are upset about Cal slowly detaching himself, maybe we should shift our perspective. We've been blessed to have Cal raise-up our city, but it's still very similar to the town he grew up in. He's seen all there is to see and as both a human being and a businessman, it's time for Cal to move on. He's made some tremendous changes for us and we will feel the effects of those for a long time. They may come to us in different forms, like smaller youth baseball tournaments or a new owner for the Ironbirds who has some ideas to shake things up and fill the seats. If anything, Cal is expanding the Ripken empire with his new facilities in Myrtle Beach and Pigeon Forge, Tennessee, which offer more tourist attractions for ball players and their families. Aberdeen can't offer beaches or mountains or amusement parks like they can. When it comes down to it, other than our friendly faces, the most special thing about Aberdeen is the Ripken family legacy. We are grateful to them, especially Cal, for the nest they have created here for future baseball stars, boys not unlike my own, in a humble little place called Aberdeen.

For my dad, Bob Chrest

She Just Wanted to Play

RACHEL PFENNIG HALES

The game was simple. Catch the ball. Don't flinch. Don't ever cry. Throw it back, harder than it came.

Thhhhhhhwack!

The sound alone was hard. There was no guessing when a regular round of catch might morph into Hard Ball, but once it did, there was no going back. The game was not mean, but intense, the way they imagined the professionals might compete. Each pitch landing with a swift, deliberate smack. The speed of the ball and the snap of the catch would just feel different. Intentional. A challenge extended, and the game would start.

Neither wanted to quit first. Actually, neither wanted to quit at all. It was fun, throwing the ball around. Even when palms stung and shoulders ached, they'd keep playing catch. Numbers two and three of what would be a family of six kids, they were often left to entertain each other. They'd stand for hours in the yard, or the street, whipping the baseball between them. Sometimes Big Brother might even pull his hand from his glove and make a big show of shaking it loose. It was a small gesture of sportsmanship to keep the tone friendly, even if it hadn't hurt. Especially if it had.

Sometimes they'd pretend it was a run for the pennant, or they were warming up for the World Series. Maybe they'd take turns moderating, like the announcer would in the big leagues. Once a year, the whole family went to a game. They ate hot dogs and cheered on their team and listened to each play live, echoing through the loud speakers. They'd pay attention to every detail, and recreate it in front of the house:

Coming up to the mound is the best young pitcher we've ever seen. An astounding career average ERA of .001. Not even Mickey Mantle can hit against this arm. The wind up. The pitch. The crowd goes wild.

Sometimes they'd pull out the strong, wooden bat. Maybe they'd have friends join and run some bases. Maybe they'd even keep score. But, mostly,

130

they played catch. It didn't matter what else was happening. If there had been a bad grade on a test, or a fight with Dad, or if Mom was pregnant with another little sister. From after school until it got dark, and as much as they could on weekends, the two played.

Back and forth. Throw and catch. Him to her. Her to him. It's how she remembers her childhood: with a baseball, a mitt, and Big Brother, throwing the ball.

* * *

They put her at home plate because she was small. Not for her age, of course. She had always been tall, and could easily pass for 11, or 12 even. But compared to most of the teenagers she played with, eight years old did seem little.

The New Jersey Park Districts had just started their first competitive female league—a softball team for youth under 18. They weren't sure it would catch on but agreed to give field time to anyone who showed up. There weren't a lot of options for girls who wanted to play sports in 1960s South Brunswick. Women's sports weren't introduced in most schools until the early 1970s, and extracurricular leagues were rare.

Her brother had been playing Little League for three seasons already, and she'd been dreaming of having a team of her own. She'd have a position; there would be plays to learn; maybe she'd even get a hat with a logo and a matching shirt. If she wanted to play, this was her chance.

There was a good turnout that first year. More than expected, enough to organize a few games, though nowhere near enough for separate divisions. Most of the girls looking for a team were in high school. They were strong, athletic and starved for an opportunity to compete. She was eight and the youngest by four years. Still, the policy stated that any female under eighteen who showed up could play.

It's not that she didn't like playing catcher. Elston Howard was good. She'd seen him at a Yankees' game once. He was an all-star, and an impressive player. She knew that, in a pinch, a whole game could come down to what happens at home plate. But she also knew that's not why they put her there. Throwing and catching were simple enough, and the pitcher could run in to make any big plays. She didn't like playing catcher, because it was the big kids' way of making sure she wouldn't play at all. She was just a skinny little kid. No one trusted that she could keep up.

Still, she was on a team. They only had one game a week and didn't have organized practice, but she practiced. Every day after school, she'd make her brother stand in as pitcher. He'd throw strikes. He'd throw balls. He'd throw wild, unpredictable curves he'd claim were intentional. She dove and she slid. She crouched behind the divot they'd dug in the lawn and dubbed home base.

If she were going to be a catcher, she'd be the best in South Brunswick Girls' Softball history.

Her big moment came about halfway through the season. A double play at the end of the game … it happened fast … miss in the outfield … tag out at second … runner from the other team charging toward home. Beyond catching strikes, she hadn't seen much action at home plate. This was what she had been practicing for. The catcher was ready. She waited for the ball. She guarded the plate.

But the pitcher saw the play too. The hit. The miss. A big girl—tall with wide shoulders and a long gait, she was the self-declared captain. As soon as the ball cracked off the bat, the pitcher sprung into action. She came barreling in toward home, glove out and ready to make the catch. This could be the game winning moment.

But more, this could be the catcher's only real play of the season. The catcher knew that. That little girl, still young enough to show her age in fingers, wanted to win. That skinny little girl who taught herself how to play needed to prove her spot on the team. That headstrong little athlete, who would eventually grow up to be my mother, took both hands and shoved her own pitcher out of the way.

No one was expecting it. Especially not my mom. She didn't get in fights, and she didn't push giant mean girls twice her age and size. She blames adrenaline. The excitement of the moment. Calls it practically out-of-body. But, she caught the ball. She tagged the runner out. She ended the game. Swift and seamless, she was a natural.

The pitcher shook her head, looking up to the catcher from her spot in the dirt. Mom had made the play. The pitcher couldn't deny it. No one could. The team had a catcher.

* * *

I know the story well. My mom, the two-sport varsity athlete, in the first years that was even an option, fighting for fair treatment in the graduation policy at her high school. She hadn't set out to do that, of course. If they hadn't been threatening her own diploma, she may not have noticed that male and female athletes had different physical education requirements. Still, she was a crusader, and baseball was her platform.

Mom's family had moved from New Jersey to Chicago as she was starting her freshman year in the fall of 1973. They lived on a good block, in a good community. Her high school sat high up on a hill, surrounded by decades-old trees and a lake where people gathered for fireworks every Fourth of July. It was picturesque, and Mom liked it there, once she stopped being new.

The biggest problem was that the new high school didn't have any competitive women's teams. But neither did the school in New Jersey. There was cheerleading club, and archery club, and a new activities room they called the girl's gym. The gender-segregated physical education curriculum asked girls to bounce basketballs, swing rackets for tennis, and, for two weeks out of every semester, play catch. Mom hadn't been on an actual team for a few years. It wasn't easy liking baseball as a girl in the 1970s.

But things were changing. The year before the big move, in 1972, the United States Department of Education passed Title IX of the Education Amendments. It "prohibits discrimination on the basis of sex in any federally funded education program or activity." Mom didn't understand the significance of the law and can't even remember if it was big news when President Nixon signed the bill. Still, it meant that if schools were going to use government funding, they had to provide equivalent activities for both boys and girls. It meant that, by Mom's junior year, there would be two varsity women's sports, basketball and softball, and she would participate in both.

Practice was held after school. There were two or three games per week. They had green and white uniforms and traveled by bus to other schools in the division. She played first base. She waxed her glove after practice. She was an athlete, by all definitions of the word.

School policy stated that in-season athletes could forego gym class to study or work, as needed. Always a strong student, Mom didn't need the extra time for homework, but as one of six kids, she did need to make some money if she wanted to attend college. There was no time for a steady job after school, as basketball season rolled into softball, so she paired her study hall and physical education class together, and went to work at the local gas station for two hours every school day.

Mom is very clear: this was not something she was hiding from teachers, or using as an excuse to cut class. She knew the policy for athletes, and was making good use of her time. She'd wave at the hall monitors as she walked out the tall front doors of the school. She'd walk up the block, put on her gas attendant's smock, and pump gas for all her parents' friends. She specifically remembers the principal stopping in twice a week and always commenting on the hard working nature of his students. This is how varsity players got it all done, and she was grateful for the time. Until the last day of school her senior year.

Mom was called into the main office the day before she planned to walk across the gymnasium stage and get her diploma. It seemed she did not have enough physical education courses to graduate. She had not been attending gym class. If she wanted to move onto college, the school needed her to come back over the summer.

This part of the story is always embellished. Depending on who's telling it, my mom comes across as a bra-burning feminist, a warrior of women's rights, and an all-together badass activist. When she tells it the story is much quieter. She never set out to fight for anything. She didn't mean to be on the front lines, demanding equality. She just needed to graduate high school. But on the horizon of a new era for women, my mom did all those things.

She sat strong, and stoic in the principal's office. Not a single boy was having their pre-requisites questioned before graduation. Boys' sports were determined to be physically active enough that gym class wasn't an added necessity. But not girls' sports? Mom took a deep breath. Looking the principal in the eye, she mustered all her courage and said, "This isn't right." The school allowed the boys flexibility in their schedules, and had for years. If that was the policy for varsity athletes, that should apply to both male and female players.

She wanted fair treatment, and eventually, she got it.

My whole life I've heard about my mom, the bold crusader. The woman who fought her way to the diploma and ensured equality at her high school for generations to come. When you talk to her, though, the story is simple. My mom, the athlete, just wanted to play, same as the boys.

* * *

Baseball made my mom a feminist. Of course she didn't know that at the time. She just liked to play. She likes to watch. She likes to share in the experience. But it's more than that. My mom's a baseball freak because no matter where you come from, or who you are, if you play well, you can win.

I never spent much time on sports. My high school had ten sports teams dedicated to female athletes, plus several intramural clubs, training groups and recruitment connections. I had my choice of activities, and ended up in drama. I did some student council, choir, and a few leadership programs, but nothing that would put me in a uniform or connect me to a team. Still, baseball was always a part of life in our house. We'd play catch (and sometimes Hard Ball.) The garage had bats and balls and I knew how to run bases. When my daughter was born, a small, pink mitt was her very first gift from Grandma.

My mom doesn't play anymore. She walks, rides her bike, golfs, watches birds while she hikes, but she hasn't been on a baseball team in years. There was never a point where she knew she'd stop playing. Life just kept changing. She kept getting busier, and older, and she just stopped. But still, at barbecues or family reunions, if the right game starts, Mom will join in. When given the choice, Mom will always choose to play.

Big Ed

The Ballplayer in Decline

STEPHEN KIRK

When we visit him at the old folks' place, my wife always makes me enter first, in case he's sitting there in his underpants. Congestive heart disease, pulmonary fibrosis, and diabetes head the roster of my father's ailments. His cardiologist told me that when he listens to my father's breathing, it sounds like Velcro ripping. His medication list runs a full single-spaced page.

He used to be fond of referring to himself as "Big Ed," though he's never been big in any regard except girth. He's on diuretics and frequently has to rouse from bed to urinate. During a recent spate of late-night falls en route to the bathroom, it took three nurses to get him off the floor. His back is so bad that he doesn't stand upright behind his walker, but rather bends and rests his forearms on it. Going down the hall to the dining room like that, he's only waist high.

But toss him something while he's sitting in his chair and it's clear he still has good hands.

He didn't start golfing until he was in his fifties, when he'd already lost some flexibility. Despite a swing worse than any this side of Charles Barkley's, he kept himself in pocket money over the next twenty years, beating up on the other old guys. He had a couple of holes in one, and the plaques on his wall to prove it.

Baseball, however, was and always will be his game. The regret he expresses most often is that he can no longer travel to Florida for Spring Training. He's an Atlanta Braves fan, but any televised Major League game will do. If not that, college ball. Or women's softball. Or the Little League World Series.

At the end of World War II, my father was the ace pitcher on a couple of New York State championship teams—one high school and the other a

Kiwanis League, which was a big deal in his day, when baseball was king. It was a *Hoosiers*-type story of a collection of good athletes in a nothing town. Teams from the rural Finger Lakes are rarely competitive against New York City and Long Island squads. My father's Kiwanis teams competed for two seasons with only nine players on the roster.

I've seen pictures of my father in his baseball gear and in his army uniform in Korea, puffing a cigar, and he looks like a hellion. His third-biggest opportunity as a pitcher came when he was supposed to match up against Rochester's Johnny Antonelli, who a couple of years later received the biggest signing bonus to that point in baseball history. Antonelli went on to become a two-time twenty-game winner in the Major Leagues and a six-time All Star. Batting against him in the top of the first, my father was tossed from the game.

"I told the ump he needed glasses," he says.

I'm not surprised. His team won anyway.

His second-best opportunity had happier results, when he took the mound at Ebbets Field for the state high school championship. It was a practice day for the Brooklyn Dodgers, who signed baseballs for my father's team, the notable exception being Pee Wee Reese, who was too busy or preoccupied or arrogant, and whom my father disparages to this day. My father recently asked for that ball, which I recall saving when I cleaned out his house but can't locate at present. I hope I find it for him.

It was my father's first time in New York City, nearly 300 miles from home. The team stayed at the New York Athletic Club. Hayseed that he was, my father had likely never before seen an indoor track. He had an inkling he was making a mistake when he ran himself ragged doing laps on the club's track the night before the game—and felt it more acutely when the team arrived at Ebbets Field.

But maybe fatigue took the edge off what he says was the greatest nervousness he's ever experienced. He walked the first batter, who promptly stole second. My father picked him off, and it was smooth sailing from there. He pitched a complete game—seven innings for a high-school contest. The score was 5–1 or 5–2. He's not sure.

He was contacted by a scout. Late the following winter, the St. Louis Cardinals put him on a train to Georgia for a tryout. My father was out of throwing shape. His town was snowbound. He had little chance to prepare except for a couple of sessions inside the local armory. But this was his big chance. In trying to impress the Cardinals' staff, he hurt himself the first day in Georgia. He was just beginning to feel himself when the camp ended. The Cardinals shipped him home by bus, unsigned. That's a major point for my father, one he mentions every time he tells the story—down by train, back by bus.

He bears the team no resentment and indeed rooted for the Cardinals for many years. He attributes his failure to youth and inexperience and excitement. Among my father's best qualities are his honesty and modesty. He says he wasn't big-league material anyway. He estimates that, adjusted to today's classification system, he was probably a Double A–level talent.

One of my favorite anecdotes about him concerns his courtship of my mother. His baseball success made him a big deal locally. His championships and professional tryout were well covered in the local paper. But my mother went to the Catholic high school and was oblivious to sports. They'd been dating for some time when someone finally asked her, "Say, isn't he the ballplayer?" He'd never mentioned it.

If I'm any indication, men have changed as much as baseball since the 1940s. My father's life has been more momentous than mine, and I suspect I'll never have the caliber of memories he does, good or bad. He saw men killed, maimed, and badly traumatized in Korea. He was even one of those poor sods given the duty of walking a minefield and probing the ground with a metal-pointed stick. And yes, he found live mines that day.

*   *   *

My older brother had the body type and the quick throwing motion of a catcher, as my father recognized. But he wanted to play shortstop. What would seem to be a minor difference of opinion was a bitter issue in our house. I recall seeing a picture of my brother in a Little League uniform, but he didn't play long. Plenty of water has passed under the bridge since then, but I suspect that old stalemate continues to contribute to their poor relations 50-odd years later.

It took a long time for it to dawn on me, but my brother had more backbone than I did. My father coached my Little League teams from tee ball onward. He had a better eye for picking players than did the other coaches. The last couple of years especially, we practiced longer, better, and more often than the other teams. My father pitched all the batting practice, which cut down on the catcher's having to chase the ball to the backstop so often. He tailored his pitching to challenge each boy without scaring him. But most importantly, he adopted a strategy of taking on as his assistant coach the father of the premier player in the league—the kid who was bigger and stronger and more mature than everyone else and threw hard enough to induce pants-peeing in our opponents. We lost only a single game my 11- and 12-year-old seasons combined. I was the second or third pitcher on those teams. I finally discarded all my trophies when I cleaned out my parents' house.

But it was always my father's sport, not mine. I didn't hate it, but I wasn't fond of it either—something that, unlike my brother, I can't express to him to this day. When I finally escaped my father's tether, I quit in my second year of Babe Ruth ball, at age 14. That, too, became a subject of contention far beyond what it should have been. Baseball may have been a bonding experience from his perspective, but not from mine. He wanted me to be good, or at least to love the game as he did. I wasn't and didn't. His many fine qualities notwithstanding, my father is a selfish man.

We continued playing catch through high school and my summers home from college, always at his instigation, not mine. I never could turn him down.

Him: 53 years old, 5'8", comfortably beyond 200 pounds.
Me: 21, 6'4", 195.
Him: Could have broken my catching hand if he wanted.
Me: Couldn't crack a pane of glass.

We had a large backyard. Whenever he wanted to play catch, I asked that we do it there. But we always threw right in the middle of the street in front of the house, even though that meant we had to pause and move when cars passed. I don't think he meant to make a public display of his relationship with his son, or certainly to make me look bad in comparison to him. My best guess is that he wanted people to see he was still a pitcher.

Years later, after he'd moved several states away, my father learned that his hometown was starting a sports hall of fame. Save for his letters to my mother from Korea, I've never known him to put pen to paper, but he made an exception here—not on his own behalf, but on that of his old coach. That coach wasn't much of a baseball man. His players sometimes had to instruct him in strategy. But they loved him and would do anything for him. And considering the town's paucity of state titles, I have to think my father made at least a decent case for his coach. But in the tradition of Podunks everywhere, if you're not part of the in crowd, you're nobody, even if you were once a star athlete. He never received even a courtesy response.

*   *   *

Many Atlanta Braves night games are broadcast again the next day. My father sometimes doesn't realize he's watching the same game twice.

"The scheduling is terrible," he says. "They play too damn many games."

He looks at me with mild suspicion when I clarify for him that the Braves have had two managers since Bobby Cox, and that Cox has not been demoted to coaching the Triple A team.

Though he sits all day with the remote in his lap, he can't manage to find a game unless it's on one of the four or five channels he always watches. Occasionally, he calls me to ask what channel he needs. But he spent his working career in the din of a machine shop and denied his advancing deafness for so long that it's now only marginally correctible even with his hearing aids, so he can't hear my answer no matter how loudly I holler it into the phone.

*   *   *

I haven't followed baseball since before the two leagues split into three divisions each. I'd struggle to say which teams are in which divisions.

I don't know the players beyond the major stars and eight or ten Braves.

I don't have four hours to invest in a game.

I couldn't watch one even if I wanted, since I subscribe to only the basic cable package, which doesn't include the channels that broadcast baseball.

Regardless, it seems that I'm now my father's source and his lifeline.

Resume Play

Elizabeth Scott Leik

I squat down and push the glove tighter to the inside corner. A good catcher always squats, never kneels, making it easier to throw to second or third. But my arm has weakened and the ball doesn't reach second or even the pitcher if I don't stand up with the throw. My 30-year-old body reaches out for my 12-year-old Little League mentality in order to call an accurate game, as a strong catcher would, ready for each pitch. "Hit the glove!" I'd yell to the pitcher back then, pounding my fist in the catcher's mitt—a phrase that rang in my ears throughout elementary school, into college and grad school, after marriage and the birth of my daughter. "Hit the glove!" people would demand of me, and I would acquiesce, pegging the ball in some distant direction despite my fading accuracy.

"Hit the glove," I *sotto voce,* with absolutely no 12-year-old gusto, to the woman on the mound who will pitch the next two innings. I look around at the collection of us covering the infield, pounding our gloves, shifting our feet in the dirt, looking for some reconnection to each other and the game. A woman steps up to the plate, and I settle in despite the uncertainty, hoping to catch what is thrown to me.

The game unfolds before me—the structure of the field, the placement of the players, the slight shift of the infielders and outfielders depending on the batter. In the past, I knew where the ball was going with each play and called out the game. "Runner on second, get the out at first!" when we were up by a few runs. "Home first or closest to you!" when bases were loaded and we were looking for at least one out, maybe a double play if we were lucky. My job was to guide everyone so that the easiest play was made to keep us from losing the game. I did this for the team at 12, and I will try to do this now for our weekend baseball experiment. Somewhere along the way, unfortunately, I haven't quite figured out how to call a good game for myself.

*   *   *

I was in between kids, looking for something to salve the wounds of growing up, tired of the games being played around me, when I found a baseball weekend at a small, holistic camp in the Catskills. Among the courses of meditation and finding the "true you" was a class offered by two former All-American Girls Professional Baseball League players, Wilma "Briggsie" Briggs and Jean "Dutch" Louise Geissinger Harding, both from the Ft. Wayne Daisies. The League, which ran from 1943–1954, placed women on traveling teams to keep baseball in the forefront while the men served abroad during World War II. Their games started out as a version of softball that gradually took on the full baseball form and showcased women's abilities in batting, throwing, and catching. A few years earlier, the film *A League of Their Own* had been released, revealing the lost history of many of the original players, including Jean and Wilma, who were taking their past on the road, bringing women back on the field and sharing what worked for them years ago. The weekend promised general ball playing and devotion to the grace and respect of the sport. This last offering gave me hope. Through work and marriage and recent motherhood, I slowly had been losing the skills needed to navigate the world. Baseball, a game of precision set on a field of relevance, would return this to me.

About 20 years earlier, my small Pennsylvania town bent to the Title IX requirement that girls be allowed to participate in all boy sports. That February, my mother drove me to the mall and signed me up for Little League at a small table placed just below a spiral staircase that belied the fallacies in that town. The mall fountain sprinkled in the background, cleansing nothing. I recognized the men taking registrations, I had watched them coach Little League for years, played backyard ball with many of the boys who were on their teams. They sat at the table and smiled when my mother filled out the forms and wrote the check for the season, but they had already limited me. At 11, I could play only two summers. The 13- to 15-year-old senior league was not open to girls, yet. Even in the 8–12 league, I would be relegated to the minors, not drafted to the more skilled major teams run by coaches whose boys might actually have a future in baseball.

Still, I was game.

Time spent with boys would be a respite from the teasing and whispering and pettiness of certain girls who did more than frown on those who were not like them. Boys welcomed me into their games and activities no matter how I dressed or how I talked or how many times I lost or won. Playing ball turned into a lifetime of escape from backstabbing and exclusion. Years later when I read Margaret Atwood *Cat's Eye* and *Robber Bride*, I understood how many women had to look for a game to give them peace of mind in their lives.

"You know, it's like we intentionally want to stop ourselves from getting ahead," a friend told me one day over drinks.

"I work hard to separate myself from most women," I told her.

"Too hard," she replied. I nodded. Baseball taught me how to get around on a certain field—outrun the throw of hearing how ugly your outfit is at school that day; get under the tag of your female boss admitting she will never promote you because you might take her job from her. These experiences slowed up my game and made me question each play. By marriage, I realized I hadn't quite built up enough armor to defend myself. The chest protector, the shin guards, the helmet and mask—none of this deflected the barbs thrown at my psyche over the years. The equipment, I eventually learned, is merely an illusion.

"Hit the glove!" I yell with more conviction as the batter sets herself in the box. Before we started a unified game, Jean and Wilma warmed us up with some pepper and encouraging discussion. "Play any position you want, we'll rotate every two innings," Wilma told us. "And if the weather holds out through tomorrow, we'll get two or three games in." They took time to review the rules; some women admitted to never playing. "Baseball is everyone's game," they assured us.

I consider this pre-game warm up as the batter takes a few swings.

The pitcher shakes off my request for a fastball, then winds up and throws in one continuous movement. The batter watches the ball into my glove. "No balls and strikes called yet, just swing at a good one, something you like," Wilma yells. "Remember to swing your body, not just your arms!" Jean adds. The next pitch comes in and Crack!! Bat hits ball, ball jumps out to infielder, we all stop. It worked. The batter connected, the fielder picked it up, and we are a bit stunned. Someone yells, "Nice hit!" and a few of us smile. Jean claps her hands, shaking her head up and down quickly. "That's it, that's it! Go ahead, run on the next one." The batter, incorporating her desire for the game, hits a slow roller to the short stop and makes it to first before the throw.

Everyone cheers. My father, sitting under a nearby tree, looks up from his coffee and the *New York Times* and smiles, checking to see where we stand in this game. That he would drive me to upstate New York to watch me play shows his continual belief in me, even if mine has dissipated. Each skill he taught me reinforced the purpose of the game.

Throw: Lift your lead foot. Bring the arm down, around, and over as you turn your body halfway, then forward with the release, to give the ball some movement.

Hit: Run with your head down to stay focused.

Slide: Get under the tag or force the ball to drop.

Catch: Put your hand behind the glove for reinforcement.

Field: Put yourself in front of the ball. Follow it on the bad hop.

Balk: Use in any situation you don't have a handle on.

His precision created my love for the game. The feeling that runs through my body when I swing and connect with the ball, sending it over the shortstop's head on the fly or through the second baseman's legs with an in-the-dirt bounce. The sound the ball makes when it hits the glove—Thwack—such a satisfying achievement gripped tightly in my hand. Other fathers had their sons to play catch. My dad had me. It would be a few years before my younger brothers could play, but he didn't want to waste any time. He wanted to make sure I learned the game correctly. "It's all about following through," he told me, on the pitch, the catch, the hit, the run. Follow through on everything and the game will go smoothly for you.

I stopped following through in about seventh grade. I was tired of trying to keep up with a tenuous friendship that came with outlandish conditions. The rules were pretty straight forward to me—infield fly rule, an out; foul ball bunt on the third strike, an out—but they didn't really mean much to others. The emotional wear and tear placed me on the disabled list for years.

* * *

Wilma yells encouragement while clapping her hands, "That's a hit! Next batter." Jean speaks to the pitcher, twisting her hand to show how to throw a curve ball. A tall woman with a kind smile and a strong swing steps up to the plate. I crouch down to resume play. Our field is not unified with perfect lines leading off to the right and left determining fair and foul and where to stand around the plate, as they are in the big leagues. We feel lucky to have a field this weekend. Our innate skills reveal where we fit in and how this game will be played.

When we return to our bunks that Saturday night, I feel accomplished. After the vegetarian dinner, I decide to wander through the camp's small bookstore and find Susan E. Johnson's *When Women Played Hardball*, a title that makes me smile slyly because aren't we always playing hardball on some field or another? The book is a beautiful collection of research and interviews with the former players for the All-American Girls Professional Baseball League. Johnson lets these players tell their stories, bouncing off each other in detailed memory, their voices coming through with strong reflections of the game. Wilma is featured in one of the chapters, where she admits how much confidence she gained playing baseball in the League.

I need this book.

Our games end on Sunday afternoon. The two pros sign our gloves and books and tell a few more stories. They talk about what *A League of Their Own* has done for women's roles in the sport. I remember going to see the movie a few weeks before the birth of my first daughter, thrilled to think that baseball could be in my life again, even if vicariously. Near the end of the film, two players duke it out for the season finale. Dottie, the catcher, tries to set up her kid sister Kit, now on another team, in a strike out. "High fast balls. She can't hit 'em, can't lay off 'em," Dottie tells the pitcher, who throws two pitches that quickly earn easy strikes. Kit exchanges a look with Dottie that begs, 'Have you sold me out?' On the third pitch, Kit readjusts and connects with a ball out of her reach and sends it into a gap in the outfield. She takes off around the bases, and as she rounds third, against the coach's advice, she heads towards her sister, determined to even the score but also win the game. I want to yell, "Slide! Get under the tag!" but Dottie is standing in front of home plate already, holding the ball, leaving Kit with no other option but to crash into her, which she does with great force.

The ball falls out of the catcher's hands into the dirt.

The runner scores.

Two sisters, two women, two different teams.

One wins. One loses.

A game well played.

Base-Bawling

JEAN C. O'BRIEN

It was the late 1950s, and as my family walked up the slight incline so common to baseball parks, I clung to my mother's hand tightly. As we came to the summit of the walkway at Cleveland Municipal Stadium and exited from the building into the sunshine, I looked down and exclaimed, rather loudly, "Mom! THE GRASS IS GREEN!" I had embarrassed her, and I remember her yanking my hand and scolding me soundly. However, I'm pretty sure that this episode in no way diminished my enchantment with the game that followed.

My family enjoyed watching sports. Basketball, football, and baseball were the regulars on our old black-and-white television sets. Being young and dumb, for some reason the color of the playing fields didn't register as anything but the dull grey so common to all of our 1950s television experiences.

I don't know exactly the year when I first viewed the movie, *It Happens Every Spring*. Ray Milland played the lead role of the quirky chemistry professor turned pitcher, and, of course, due to its vintage, had been filmed in black and white. Paul Douglas played his usual second-banana role as the loyal catcher, which helped "hook" me into my love of this film. However, it was the theme of baseball that drew me to the movie.

I also don't remember the reason that I had fallen in love with baseball, but fall in love I had. Elementary school children are often asked, "What do you want to be when you grow up?" I remember my response to this question: "I want to turn into a boy and become Willie Mays." Ahem. Well? I simply didn't envision any other options. Unfortunately, I was gifted with exactly zero physical capabilities even to play girls' softball. I tried—oh yes, I tried— I played my very hardest in physical education classes, I joined the Girls' Athletic Association (to improve my skills), I joined a summer softball league. Nothing helped.

I collected baseball cards. I wore a baseball jacket (until it no longer fit on my young adolescent body) with patches from all of the Major League teams on the front, back, and sleeves. I had my own ball and glove. I practiced throwing and catching with my brother until he refused further participation. Never could I hit the proverbial "broad side of a barn door" with my pitches. My catching was pretty bad, too. Batting? Forget it.

Can you imagine how I felt when *A League of Their Own* appeared in our culture? These women were actually playing professional baseball during my young lifetime. How is it that nobody ever notified me of this phenomenon? Of course, there was no Internet when I was five years old, and I guess it's possible that my parents had no inkling of the existence of the All-American Girls' Professional Baseball League. Nevertheless, upon my first (and all subsequent) viewing of this film, I wept tears of joy. Yes, yes—I understand that it was a highly fictionalized version of the real thing—but somehow, it didn't matter. The truth is that girls—women—played baseball, they played it professionally, they played it well and they played with the deep love and enthusiasm for the game that I had been feeling inside of me all of my life.

You'll find many women weeping during romantic comedies. Not yours truly. The movies that set my tears flowing are those iconic baseball films. Yes, I've seen every single one of them, and yes, they all make me cry. My husband just shakes his head.

Anyone who knows me knows all about my obsession. One of my friends brought me a vial of dirt from the real "Field of Dreams" that she scored on a family vacation in Iowa. Other friends know how to tempt me for an outing—offer me baseball tickets! Acquaintances from church invited me to a Great Lakes Loons game several years ago. It was "Mickey Lolich Night." YES! I purchased a baseball, stood in line for an hour and a half, presented the ball to him for an autograph, then proceeded to put forth my left hand, saying, "I want to shake the hand that won it for us in '68." Somehow I managed to grab Don Drysdale's autograph when my family visited Florida in the '60s. During another of our Florida vacations, the Kansas City Athletics stayed at the same motel where we were. (The things one remembers when one is obsessed.)

During the 1980s a song became popular: "Center Field." My (then) husband played in a band that had a regular gig at one of the local bars. They learned this song, as they kept up with what was on the Top 40 list at the time. I didn't hang out at the bar on a regular basis, but whenever I entered this place when the guys were playing, they immediately swung into "Center Field." To this very day the song primes the pump and I become a weeping mass of jelly once again.

When my daughter was two years old, my Detroit Tigers had an incredible season, culminating in their 1984 World Series win. She learned to sing the National Anthem at this young age, hearing it so frequently on the radio. To my surprise, however, she did not develop the same love for the game as I had—until she was a young adult living in Boston during their World Series win. Even though she had previously expressed absolutely no interest in the game, when the celebratory parade passed right in front of her apartment, she turned on her cell phone, called me, held it up, and gave me a running commentary as to who was in what vehicle in front of her, whose hand she had shaken, etc., knowing that I would get a charge out of it. She also called me one year during the July 4th celebration on the Charles River to tell me that someone was reciting "Casey at the Bat" for one of the entertainment numbers. Yes, everyone knows.

At the top of my bucket list used to be: (1) Visit old Yankee Stadium; (2) Watch a game at old Yankee Stadium; (3) Watch a World Series game at old Yankee Stadium. I wanted to breathe the air that those greats of the game had breathed; I wanted to feel the dirt and sit in the seats; I wanted to hear the echoes of the roar of the crowd and the smack of the bat; I wanted to smell the hotdogs and peanuts. Sitting here typing these words brings tears to my eyes. Go figure. My current bucket list still features attending a World Series game. I now prefer that this happen at Comerica Park when the Tigers win it again.

There are not many of the "old" ballparks left. My daughter graciously has taken me to Fenway many times, and it's always a thrill to be in the place where some of those old timers played over the years. But I do miss Tiger Stadium. I know, I know. Bigger and better are the concepts for the 21st century. Comerica Park is lovely, even though I have yet to explore all of its statuary, all of its nooks and crannies. I held out for many years before consenting to attend a game there. When I finally went in 2014, it felt almost like coming home. I however made the mistake of sitting in the upper deck, right in front of a Plexiglas barrier that didn't quite come up to my waist. Now, there I had a problem. I am terrified of high places, especially those that don't (quite) give me a barrier against falling to my death. You see I am a loud and boisterous fan. When something happens, I tend to jump up and cheer. It was the bottom of the ninth, the Tigers were behind four-one, and there was not much hope for a comeback win. Although the seats had largely emptied, all the die-hard fans were hanging in there, hoping against hope for one of those miracles. We got one on, then two on, and then the bases were loaded, and Rajai Davis approached the plate. He socked a homer into the left-field seats— Grand Slam! My instinct was to jump up—and I found that I was afraid to do that. Instead, I knelt down in front of my see-through "fence" and yelled my approval until my voice gave out completely. Future games have found me seated in the lower deck behind the dugout. It gives me some measure of security while affording me a better look at the players and the field. Finances used to dictate where I could sit, but since I am now older my plastic is stronger.

The thrill is still there. I am now 65 years old and when I walk down the concrete steps and can smell the hotdogs, when I take my seat so close to the field that I can almost touch the grass, when I see the expressions on the players' faces and can hear their banter, my eyes become very wet and once again, I am home.

PART III

The Post-Season

October is truly the time when our baseball fandom is tested. Some of us don't ever get to experience the glory of winning the World Series. Sometimes our teams spend years stinking ... or they don't quite make it ... or they get all the way to the ultimate, the World Series, and lose.

But none of us would give up the post-season spectacle. The fate of our individual team favorites doesn't diminish our baseball love. If we can't root for our own team, most of us have second-favorite teams, or third. We might pull for a favorite player—we can even wish loudly and mightily for the demise of a despised opponent.

Baseball works for us. It has a beginning, a middle, and an end. It's dependable, reliable, and timeless. Thank you, baseball.

Maz's Homer

JOSEPH BATHANTI

Pittsburgh. 1960. October 13. A Thursday. In the final inning of what will be, by anyone's measure, a mythic World Series, the hometown Pittsburgh Pirates battle a venerable unbeatable New York Yankees team that will go on to play in the next four World Series: Mickey Mantle, Roger Maris, Yogi Berra, Elston Howard, Whitey Ford, Casey Stengel.

Two months past my seventh birthday, I am in the second grade at Saints Peter and Paul School on Larimer Avenue, a street that cradles my family's identity in the new world. Sister Ann Francis, my teacher, whom I do not like at all, though she will not prove the worst of them, slips us word that Sister Geralda, the ferocious school principal, who also teaches eighth grade, has granted amnesty for the last ten minutes of the school day. We are to hurry home to witness the climax of the World Series.

Does Sister Geralda like baseball? I tend to doubt it, but I know nothing about her, nothing of what beats in her heart, nothing of what distinguishes her from the cruel and catatonic night face of the steely Allegheny River when our old Plymouth rolls across it over the Highland Park Bridge. Nothing except that she paralyzes me with terror and, when I manage to cross her, she flails me unmercifully with a board.

Released, I run as fast as I can the entire way to my home on 430 Lincoln Avenue. My sister, a sixth grader, a kind and perfect girl, runs behind me. We blow in the kitchen door, whip by my mother into the living room, turn on the enormous Magnavox and fall into the couch.

Bill Mazeroski, a humble Polish-Catholic second baseman with the hands of a magician, leads off the bottom of the ninth for the Pirates. The score is 9–9. The seventh and final game of the deadlocked Series. The time is 3:36:30. Ralph Terry, the Yankees fifth pitcher of the day, is on the mound. Maz takes Terry's first pitch for a ball, then cracks the next pitch over the huge scoreboard in left field—still the only World Series-winning walk-off homer in baseball history—to win the World Championship for Pittsburgh. Church bells toll all across the city.

Never in my life have I witnessed such unadulterated celebration, such unanimous joy. The citizens of Pittsburgh stay up all night, beating on pots and pans, singing and dancing. The tunnels leading in and out of the city are impassable for the mountains of newspaper and confetti. It is a moment I will measure the rest of my life by.

That home run remains one of the mileposts of my consciousness, a Station of the Cross. Clearly a miracle. As luminous as the Burning Bush; or The Feast of the Epiphany (from the Greek: *the appearance; miraculous phenomenon*) which commemorates the "revelation of God to mankind in human form, in the person of Jesus"—when the wise men, Caspar, Melchior and Balthasar, showed up in Bethlehem. It is a Holy Day of Obligation.

Epiphany has also a decided literary valence. James Joyce, of course, "extended the meaning of the word": a "sudden, dramatic and startling [moment] which [seems] to have heightened significance and to be surrounded with a kind of magical aura."

On the day of that epiphanic home run in 1960, my father, a millwright on the Open Hearth at Edgar Thomson Steel Works in Braddock, the first steel mill that Andrew Carnegie erected in the United States, was six days away from his forty-fifth birthday. He would live to double that age and then some and, for all those years to follow, very nearly half a century, he would claim that he and I (my sister is curiously absent from his account) were at Forbes Field the day Maz launched his epic homer.

Not only that. My father also recounted, year after year, without wavering from the facts as he saw them, the following narrative. As the Pirates came to bat in their end of the ninth, I stood and made a proclamation in a voice ethereal enough to somehow compel the attention of all 36,663 fans that day swelling Forbes Field. I imagine myself enveloped in a heavenly shimmer, a sudden eerie hush befalling the minions, as they turned as one to where my dad and I sat in General Admission. I, a seven-year-old prophet, gave warning that Maz would hit it out on the second pitch. And then, by God, he did.

Well, I truly like my father's version better than mine. It's a great story, much better than what really happened. In it, I share the stage with what is arguably the most famous home run in the annals of baseball. Indeed, my father's version elevates me to the story's protagonist, a little seer who can predict miracles—nearly Messianic. And, I suppose, more than anything, I am flattered. It was a way for my father, a man who revealed through words little of what he felt, to reveal his love for me. In his version of that greatest day of all days in Pittsburgh Pirates history, the big story was not the 1960 World Series, or Bill Mazeroski, or the city of Pittsburgh. Nope. It was me, his only son, a measly seven year old, who emerged from it all a kid-prophet.

"The version we dare to write is the only truth, the only relationship we can have with the past," writes Patricia Hampl. Which is true—unless we accept others' versions of the past. Like my father's.

But my father's version, if one may dispute a memory, is a figment. I was sitting on the couch next to my sister at our home on Lincoln Avenue. Yes, I watched that ball sail over Yogi Berra's head and into Schenley Park. But I watched it on television.

Furthermore, my father would have never taken a day off from work to go to a ballgame. To do so, he would have lost eight hours pay, and forked out who knows how much for World Series tickets. He simply was not constituted thusly, period; and under no circumstances would my parents have allowed me to skip school for a ball game. I saw more baseball at Forbes Field with my dad than any other father-son duo I can drum up, but we were absolutely not at that one.

I don't know how many times my father recounted that story over the years—dozens—but I never once contradicted him. As much out of love and respect as anything. My father was pretty much the nicest man I've ever met and I can say in absolute truth (a word which this piece seems bent on discrediting) that he never once in the time we spent together on earth gave me a hard time unless I forced him into it. Not one gratuitous harangue or criticism. No meddling. I cannot remember one instance of his hurting my feelings. So it just was not in me to spoil what he fervently believed and gave him such pleasure to recount.

Another thing: he never told stories. The Mazeroski-home run-prediction-story is the only story I ever heard him tell, and I felt honored to be in it. Because I never piped up to correct my father—nor did my sister, leg to leg with me that day on the couch, nor my mother, at the kitchen sink when Maz connected—my father's version of that day became family canon. The more I heard him tell it—with an uncharacteristic passionate verve, attention to detail, narratively nuanced in every way, and never differing, version to version, year in and year out—the more I began to weigh the two versions, mine and his, in terms of verisimilitude—even though, again, his version was false. Yet my dad is a supremely more credible source than I. Anyone who knew him would attest to this. I rely on lying. He had been forty-five and I a mere seven. Certainly his age bestows an authority to his memory that a second grader cannot claim.

Could I have possibly been at that game and somehow repressed that memory? Am I secretly clairvoyant? " ... not only have I always had trouble distinguishing between what happened and what merely might have happened," testifies Joan Didion, "but I remain unconvinced that the distinction, for my purposes, matters." Thus, it seems almost safe to say that I was there at Forbes Field, that I did rise and—in that gusty disembodied voice in *Field of Dreams* (a movie that, by the way, I do not like) that announces "If you build it, he will come"—predict that Maz was going downtown on the second pitch out of Ralph Terry's right hand.

In fact, I was there. The little Catholic boy, sacristan, acolyte, choir boy, in blue blazer with an emblem on his breast pocket of the Mater Dolorosa, white shirt and tie, next to a steelworker in a lime green asbestos jumpsuit and blue hardhat. That was me: the truant seven-year-old prognosticator people are still wondering what happened to.

This essay was previously published in Joseph Bathanti's book Half of What I Say Is Meaningless, *Mercer University Press (2014), and is reprinted here with the author's permission.*

Jackie

Douglas J. Butler

It was a simple act. An aging black man lobbed a baseball to a Native American catcher. They were stars of two generations. Each had received Major League Baseball's Rookie of the Year award, each was selected as the National League's Most Valuable Player and each would be a first-ballot inductee into baseball's Hall of Fame. Fifty-three thousand fans politely applauded as Johnny Bench fielded the toss and then returned the ball to Jackie Robinson, completing a pre-game ceremony honoring the 25th anniversary of Robinson's groundbreaking 1947 season. The men shook hands, then fans' attention turned to the field as the hometown Cincinnati Reds and the Oakland Athletics readied for Game Two of the 1972 World Series.

My father and I had been lucky, attending this game following a series of unlikely events: the timely reading of an out-of-town newspaper notice detailing ticket sales; promptly mailing an $81 check requesting two "strips" of World Series tickets (reserving the same seats for all four potential home games); the arrival midway through the then best-of-five National League Championship Series of the most special passes I ever held; and the improbable conclusion of the NLCS—a fifth-game, come-from-behind, ninth-inning Reds victory that began with a Bench homer and ended with George Foster scoring the winning run on a wild pitch.

Our seat location, in the highest reaches of the center field deck, was not a detraction. What mattered is that we were *there*, inside a modernist venue named Riverfront Stadium, cheering for the home team.

I was one month shy of my eighteenth birthday, a college freshman living at home. Relentless study to enter medical school had but one distraction: the Cincinnati Reds. Since moving to Ohio four months earlier, I had made once- or twice-weekly pilgrimages, often with my parents, to Riverfront Stadium, a three-year-old concrete and steel ring hugging the north bank of the

Ohio River, where for a half-dozen years in the 1970s, the Big Red Machine executed some of the best baseball ever played.

When not there in person, I tuned to WLW radio. Veteran broadcaster Joe Nuxhall (a former Reds pitcher who in 1944, at age 15, became the youngest Major Leaguer ever) and his new partner, Al Michaels, teamed for the play-by-play. But the words Reds fans cherished most were part of Nuxhall's verbal victory dance, "And this one belongs to the Reds."

Game 1 had not gone well for the home team. Ken Holtzman held Cincinnati's vaunted offense to two runs in five innings before Rollie Fingers and Vida Blue shut the Machine down for the final stanzas. Fireworks came instead from an unheralded catcher, the A's Gene Tenace, homering in his first two at bats, a Series first, en route to a 3–2 Oakland win.

As we had for Game 1, my father and I arrived nearly two hours early for the second game, entering Riverfront minutes after the gates opened. Vendors along the broad ramp to the upper deck were already hawking their wares. Cries of "hot dogs" and "programs here," echoed off the undersides of bleachers, competing with amplified tunes from a calliope and brass band aboard a riverside steamboat sporting a nearly vessel-long "Re-elect the President" banner.

Team warm-ups were in progress as we entered the stadium's inner ring. While the Big Red Machine had been the pre–Series favorite, both clubs featured outstanding talent. Oakland's roster showcased three future Hall-of-Famers, including the day's starting pitcher, Jim "Catfish" Hunter. Cincinnati fielded an equal number plus the sport's all-time "Hit King," Pete Rose, denied a place in the Hall by a lifetime ban for gambling. Both managers would be enshrined in Cooperstown as well, the A's Dick Williams and George "Sparky" Anderson of the Reds.

Little fanfare preceded Jackie Robinson's appearance, and tense negotiations leading to the event had been largely shielded from public view. I do not recall being aware that he would appear, and a digital search of the *Cincinnati Enquirer* failed to find notice of the planned presentation. Indeed the ceremony honoring Robinson's 1947 season with the Brooklyn Dodgers—which began with his becoming the first African American Major League ballplayer and ending with Rookie of the Year honors—was not unlike other presentations preceding major sporting events.

While I knew of his civil rights breakthrough, I knew little of Robinson's baseball career, which ended before my second birthday. A quarter century seems like eons to a teenager, and Robinson, the player, was lumped with stars of my father's youth. My generation's baseball heroes—Aaron and Mays, Maris and Mantle, Koufax and Clemente—were racially and ethnically diverse. The 1972 Reds, for example, typically started three foreign-born Hispanics, two African Americans, two whites, and one Native American.

But Jackie Robinson was far more complex than the non-violent, passive stereotype frequently depicted today. According to Michael Long, author of *First Class Citizenship*, Robinson was so angered that no African American had yet managed a Major League team that he at first refused to attend. As late as one week prior to the World Series, President Nixon had been scheduled to present the award, but despite entreaties from Baseball Commissioner Bowie Kuhn, Robinson relented only after a last-minute promise by Kuhn to redouble efforts to hire a black manager.

Anger was a trait that the star learned to channel effectively. Born in Cairo, Georgia, in 1919, Robinson was the grandson of a slave, son of sharecroppers and the youngest of five children. After Jackie's father abandoned the family, his mother Mallie moved her children to Pasadena, California, encountering there an informal yet still pervasive discrimination. A youthful Jackie resisted authority, briefly joining a gang and ultimately receiving a two-year suspended sentence following a 1938 arrest for verbally confronting police.

Segregation was less common in athletics, however, and Robinson competed with and against white talent. At UCLA he became the first athlete to letter in four varsity sports and won the 1940 national NCAA long jump championship.

A brief semi-professional football career ended in April 1942 when Robinson was drafted into the army. Although earning the rank of second lieutenant, he chafed under the military's rigid segregation. The officer's anger boiled over on July 6, 1944, when he was ordered to the back of an army bus. Although the order was improper, Robinson argued so vehemently with investigators as to be arrested. The following month a court-martial acquitted him of insubordination, and he was honorably discharged before year's end, never seeing combat.

In 1945, when Robinson joined the Kansas City Monarchs of the Negro League, baseball's "color barrier" was beginning to crack. In April, he and two other African American players received an ultimately unsuccessful try-out—considered by some a sham—with the Boston Red Sox at Fenway Park.

On August 28, Robinson met with Branch Rickey, general manager of the Brooklyn Dodgers. Rickey was both crusader and pragmatist. While righting a social wrong, he hoped that African American talent would lead to a Dodgers' pennant and increase attendance by the region's sizable black community. Rickey probed Robinson's character during the three-hour meeting, expressing concerns about the player's tempestuous past.

"Are you looking for a Negro afraid to fight back?" Robinson asked.

Rickey instead sought a player "with the guts not to fight back," ultimately receiving Robinson's word to "turn the other cheek" for at least three years. The signing was announced two months later; in 1946 Robinson would play for the Montreal Royals of the International League, the Dodgers' top farm club.

The white-haired man with ebony skin who walked slowly on Riverfront's AstroTurf that October afternoon could hardly be imagined as the fleet-footed athlete who opened the Dodgers' 1947 season playing first base, then for ten years anchored the league's dominant franchise. Accompanied by wife Rachel and children Sharon and David, Jackie Robinson accepted a plaque from Commissioner Bowie Kuhn commemorating the 25th anniversary of that debut season. Walter "Red" Barber, the Dodgers' radio voice during the 1940s (and a former Cincinnati Reds broadcaster) emceed the short presentation.

Robinson thanked his wife of 26 years and their children, likely remembering Jackie Jr., his eldest son, killed one year earlier in an automobile accident. His amplified words echoed around the circular stadium, however, resulting at times in a muffled, barely understandable garble. He thanked baseball and Branch Rickey for the opportunities given him then, gazing toward third base, concluded "I am going to be tremendously more pleased and more proud when I look at that third base coaching line one day and see a black face managing in baseball." A brief pause allowed those final words to be heard clearly by all.

The ceremonial first pitch followed as Robinson stood beside Kuhn in the commissioner's box.

Game 2 was another disappointment for Reds fans, however, a "flat" performance according to Pete Rose. Catfish Hunter allowed just six Cincinnati hits before Rollie Fingers, another future Hall of Famer, retired the final batter. Joe Rudi homered for the A's in the third inning, then in the bottom of the ninth, with his back to the diamond, he made a leaping catch of a Denis Menke drive, helping seal a 2–1 Oakland victory and extending the Reds' home-field World Series losing streak to seven, dating through three Series.

Descending Riverfront's ramps, I likely gave no thought to Robinson's brief appearance. While it was nice to have seen an aging star and historical icon, my mind was fixed on the disappointment of the day's main event. The next three games would be in Oakland. No team had ever rallied from an 0–2 deficit after two home losses. The Reds would need to win two of three road games or "my" World Series would be over.

My father and I exited in silence. He cherished baseball, spoke of past stars, and even though my playing skills never matched his, instilled in me a love of the game. A talented lefty raised in the anthracite-laden hills of Pennsylvania, he played first base well into his forties, competing in a rugged brand of industrial softball. As an adult he adopted the Cincinnati Reds as his team and followed the 1972 Machine with an intensity equal to mine.

The next morning, Jackie Robinson's pre-game appearance received scant media attention. The *Enquirer* included just three paragraphs—all in the body of a feature highlighting a Florida fan attending his 30th World Series—plus a single photo on the bottom of page 60.

The Reds fared better on the road, however. With late-afternoon starts and prime-time broadcasts, an innovation pioneered the preceding year, we watched nearly every pitch of the West Coast games waiting to learn if our remaining World Series tickets would be of value. The third game went to the Reds 1–0, a three-hit shutout by Jack Billingham and Clay Carroll. Oakland won the next contest 3–2, scoring two runs in the bottom of the ninth, then Cincinnati notched a 5–4 Game 5 victory with single tallies in the visitors' eighth and ninth before Joe Morgan threw out Oakland pinch runner Johnny "Blue Moon" Odom at home completing a double play to end the game.

The Series returned to Riverfront, and in Game 6 the Big Red Machine's offense—ranked by baseball historians as among the best ever—came alive with a ten-hit performance including a Bench homer, doubles by Joe Morgan and Hal McRae, and a Dave Concepcion triple. Cincinnati fans celebrated as the home team cruised to an 8–1 win, the only Series game that year decided by more than one run.

The following morning we used our final World Series ticket. This would not only be *a* World Series game, but a *seventh-and-deciding* game. A Reds win would capture the team's first championship since 1940, capping off my season as a fan with a perfect ending.

But baseball, although "just a game," can break your heart. Cincinnati never led, and after Joe Rudi squeezed a Pete Rose fly ball in the ninth, Oakland's mustachioed men mobbed one another, celebrating a 3–2 victory. Reds fans sat mute as our team—*our* Big Red Machine—fell in the October classic for the second time in three years.

My father and I again exited in silence, a rarity in our relationship that was deepening into a lifelong friendship. But while enduring a great disappointment, I knew this World Series would always rank among my most special memories. For nine days—perhaps for the final time in my life—I put daily concerns, academic worries, even thoughts of my looming Selective Service registration aside, immersing myself with a child-like innocence and a young adult's intensity into the greatest sporting event I have witnessed.

* * *

Two days later, Jackie Robinson died at his home in Stamford, Connecticut. He was 53. The ceremony at Riverfront Stadium was the final public appearance of the man who broke Major League Baseball's modern color barrier.

Hadn't I just seen him, the athlete who stole home 19 times through a storied career? And age 53 … just slightly older than my father. But the media noted Robinson's failing health while chronicling his athletic achievements and civil rights milestones. A 31-year-old Jesse Jackson gave the eulogy at a service attended by 2,500 people at Manhattan's interdenominational Riverside Church, then a funeral procession passed tens of thousands of mourners en route to Cypress Hills Cemetery just a few miles from Brooklyn's Ebbets Field.

I had little time, however, to reflect. Midterms required immediate attention and copious study. Following medical training, my lack of reflection was replaced with an increasing interest and deeper appreciation of Robinson's life. With each honor he received, I recalled that October ceremony and felt increasing amazement at having witnessed the event.

In 1982, a 20-cent U.S. postage stamp showcased a sliding Robinson stealing home below the star's portrait, the first African American athlete so honored. Two years later, President Ronald Reagan posthumously awarded Robinson the Presidential Medal of Freedom; in 1987, both Major Leagues' Rookie of the Year awards were renamed the "Jackie Robinson Award." And in 1990, Daytona Beach, Florida—where during the Dodgers 1946 spring training Robinson was not allowed to lodge with his white teammates—renamed its City Island Ballpark the Jackie Robinson Ballpark, home today of the Class A Daytona Tortugas.

However, I am equally impressed with Robinson's post-baseball life, 15 years that may have challenged the star as much as his decade with the Dodgers. In baseball he enjoyed nearly universal African American support, while his athletic prowess and personal integrity slowly mitigated racial animosity. But business, politics, and activism—in which Robinson played prominent roles—strained his tolerance and threatened his legacy.

Turmoil began even before Robinson's retirement from baseball in January 1957. Following pedestrian statistics the prior season, Walter O'Malley, now the Dodger's general manager, traded the star to the rival New York Giants, citing "the good of the team." Unbeknownst to Dodger brass, Robinson had already joined New York coffee house chain Chock Full o'Nuts as vice-president, becoming the highest-ranking African American executive of a major American corporation.

A few months later, at age 38, Robinson was diagnosed with diabetes. Although never a smoker nor drinker, hypertension and a heart attack followed, and when the Hall-of-Famer accepted the 1972 award, he was nearly blind.

Robinson's fidelity to principle resulted in shifting alliances. In 1960 both presidential candidates, Richard Nixon and John Kennedy, met with the former player seeking his endorsement, a nod given to Nixon despite objections from other black leaders. Four years later as the nation's most prominent black Republican, Robinson resigned from Chock Full o'Nuts to serve as one of six national directors for Nelson Rockefeller's Republican presidential campaign. Robinson then broke with the party at the 1968 convention, which nominated Barry Goldwater and cast his support to Democrat Hubert Humphrey over Richard Nixon.

Relationships with African Americans could be similarly testy. He distanced himself from teammate Roy Campanella over the latter's tolerance of racial taunts yet publically exchanged vitriolic letters with Malcolm X with the black separatist ultimately accusing Robinson of "still trying to win 'The Big Game' for your White Boss." In 1957 Robinson headed the NAACP's Freedom Fund Drive and for ten years served on that organization's board, while in 1960 he assisted the Student Non-Violent Coordinating Committee (SNCC) before parting ways with black radicals soon thereafter.

Meanwhile, Robinson continued reaching milestones. In 1965, he became the first black analyst on a baseball telecast; in the summer of 1972, the Dodgers retired his uniform number 42. Major League Baseball retired that number across both leagues, a first in any major sport. Two years prior to his death, Robinson launched one final endeavor—the Jackie Robinson Construction Company—to build affordable housing.

*   *   *

More than four decades later memories of "my" World Series remain etched with a clarity undimmed by time. Hits by Bench and Tony Perez, slick fielding by Concepcion and Cesar Geronimo, base running by Morgan and Bobby Tolan, and the intense play of Pete Rose made for great baseball despite a seventh-game defeat. Each October, emotions flood back as I watch broadcasts of another fall classic, recalling the Series shared with my father.

But an event barely noted at the time, today outranks the on-field play for historical significance. The ceremony's importance adds to the joy of having attended that World Series. Jackie Robinson has become for me more than a star of my father's generation or a civil rights icon; he is now part of my life, as if I had met him, which in a way I have.

Cherished totems remain: yellowed newspaper clippings; a World Series program; and eight ticket stubs arranged by date inside the envelope in which they arrived. As I hold these mementos in the early autumn of my life, recollections of an October from the springtime of that life overwhelm me: the most exciting baseball I have witnessed; a landmark event advancing racial reconciliation, and indelible memories of a father-son bond. Maybe these are some of the reasons why baseball is our national pastime.

Hey, Hey and Holy Cow

BECKY MASON STRAGAND

You've heard of the rivalry, the Crosstown Classic, the Windy City Showdown, the North Siders v. the South Siders. Yes, I'm talking about the Chicago Cubs and the Chicago White Sox. The "Lovable Losers" and the "Pale Hose."

My family has loved baseball and these two teams for at least four generations. Living in close proximity to the "City of the Big Shoulders," we had ample opportunity to watch them on the small screen, listen to the radio broadcasts and see them in person.

The trouble was, we were and are still a family divided. You see, we all didn't love both teams. No, we established our individual loyalties to either the Sox or the Cubs.

I grew up with baseball and softball in one form or another. My dad played ball and later umpired local games. My brothers played on the high school team. When I was young, I attended these games by walking along the railroad tracks to the ballpark instead of taking the long inconvenient way, known as the road lined with sidewalks. There, I watched the games sitting on a blanket on the hood of one of several cars parked around the ball field. That was the way some folks watched, since the bleachers were about ready to fall down and the danger of getting a splinter in one's backside was very real.

In the interest of transparency, I must now disclose that I am a Cubs fan. Yes, I am a member of that select group whose favorite phrase is "Maybe next year."

I must have gotten that latent gene from my grandma and grandpa on my mom's side. They loved the Cubs. Our family had a television before they did and so they would come over to our house to watch the games. One year, their children got together to buy them a set of their own and installed it while they were away. Needless to say, that surprise was a rousing success.

Grandma especially loved Jack Brickhouse, the Cubs' announcer and according to her, his word was gospel.

On to the next generation, my dad was a die-hard White Sox fan, who married my mom, daughter of the aforementioned Cubs fans. It wasn't that dad didn't try to brainwash me into his way of thinking. He had succeeded with my older siblings. Donna and Dave became Sox fans. He wasn't so lucky with us younger three kids. Poor dad, even his sister was a fan of the Cubs. He and my Aunt Violet had many spirited discussions on this subject.

He tried his best, though to sway us. He took us to games at Comiskey Park to cheer on the Sox and plied us with soft drinks and hot dogs.

One of my first memories of Comiskey was being a bit disappointed that the bullpen contained no actual animals. My sister Barb remembers the automated ball basket behind home plate that popped up when a replacement ball was needed and then disappeared into a trap door. I do not remember that. What I do remember vividly is that the park looked so huge. Coming from a small town with a population of around 600, we had never seen so many people in one place. And every baseball hit looked like it was going to fly forever and it was a bit of a shock when someone in the outfield caught it.

When the never-been-seen-before "exploding scoreboard" was installed, our only wish was that the Sox would hit a homer. They obliged, and the scoreboard rewarded the crowd handsomely with the fireworks, sound effects, and lights. Yep, we kids were mighty impressed.

Impressed, that is, until dad made the mistake of giving in to our wish to see that other Chicago team, the one that we kids saw on TV on WGN. So off we went to Wrigley Field, the "Friendly Confines." No lights for night games. No fancy scoreboard. Heck, it wasn't even automatic; they put the changing scores up by hand. But there was that clock, the organist, the ivy-covered walls, the bleachers and the bleacher bums, and the cute bear cub and the large "C" logo on their uniforms, and that iconic red sign outside the park.

That was it. That latent Cubs gene sprang to life. We turned into real fans, listening to announcer Jack Brickhouse shouting "Hey Hey!" Many years later we enjoyed Harry Caray singing (off-tune) "Take Me Out to the Ball-game" during the seventh inning stretch, and yelling "Holy Cow! Cubs Win! Cubs Win!"

My brother Tom and I were so enamored with Jack's announcing that we used our little reel-to-reel tape recorder to capture those iconic moments, so we could listen again and again. And, we just knew we would go to jail because of the announcement that the telecast was the property of Major League Baseball and any reproduction or description of the game was strictly prohibited without express written permission of the team, etc., etc. But the baseball authorities never came for us. Guess they figured that two sorry little kids with a poor recording off the TV couldn't do the Cubs much harm. And so we went on recording.

Being raised in our house meant we were all well aware of the goings-on of the Sox. Dad would watch them on TV while at the same time listen to the radio broadcast with the little transistor up close to his ear. It was hard not to absorb some of that propaganda.

My sister Barb also rooted for the Cubs, but she did stray a time or two. She remembers sending away one dollar for a pack of baseball cards. White Sox cards, that is. She also remembers that dad seemed very happy when the cards came. He must have thought that he had converted her. Those cards featured some big Sox names; Nellie Fox, Jim Landis, Early Wynn, Luis Aparicio, and Sherm Lollar. The cards were impressive but I think Barb remained true to the Cubbies.

The Cubs names of our childhood are ones we can still recite to this day: Glenn Beckert, Don Kessinger, Ron Santo (whom I had a huge crush on), Billy Williams, Ken Holtzman, Fergie Jenkins, and of course the incomparable #14, Ernie "Let's Play Two" Banks, Mr. Cub.

Those names live on in the form of a scrapbook that Tom and I made and kept. He recently sent it to me and the memories came flooding back. Just a plain brown faux leather book, but what treasures still lie within. Inside of the front cover, one of us drew and colored the circular Cubs logo. He thinks it was my work because of the precision of the drawing and I think, for the same reason, that he drew it. Maybe one of us drew and the other colored.

We lovingly filled that book with articles and photos from the regional papers. They are yellowed and brittle, and some of the tape has come off making them loose from the pages, but they hold priceless headlines including "Ernie Is Still Frisky as a Cub," "Jenkins Blanks St. Louis," and "Cub Bats Hum in 19–0 Rampage." San Diego was on the unfortunate end of that score. Apparently there was a regular short column entitled *Ernie Banks Says*. These are scattered throughout the book and as usual, Ernie was always building up his team or his teammates. There is even a Don Kessinger autograph taped to one of the pages. I think that on some cold afternoon, I will re-attach the articles and put the book back to rights. Maybe the next generation will also treasure it.

And while we are on the subject of future generations, let it be said that the divided loyalties continue. When my sister Donna, the White Sox fan, was presented with her first grandchild, Bryan, she gave him a White Sox onesie. Guess she thought that baby Bryan would become a Sox fan by osmosis. It didn't work. He grew up to become a Cubs fan and a Notre Dame fan in a family of Purdue people. In the 2005 World Series, when the White Sox swept the Astros four games to none, Donna thought that surely Bryan would cheer for her Sox just this once, what with Chicago just being up the road and all. She thought wrong. But on the other hand, Donna will not cheer for the Cubs in the World Series because she is a true and staunch American League fan. And so it goes, generation to generation.

The baseball bickering goes well beyond the realm of our immediate family. It extends to relatives of our in-laws. Yes, it casts a wide net. Consider the case of my brother-in-law, Jerry. His grandma shared a house with her two brothers. They had moved in after her husband, Jerry's grandpa, passed away. She paid for a television and asked them to share the cost. They refused, stating that they did not watch TV. Trouble was, Jerry's grandma was gone from the house two afternoons per week, once to get her hair done and once to play cards. Suspecting that something amiss was going on, suspecting that they were secretly watching baseball games, the first thing she would do upon her return home was to put her hand on the television to see if it was warm. It sometimes was. She was not going to be outsmarted. The saving grace to this was that they were all Cubs fans. At least they were all cheering for the same team.

Relatives including cousins continue to poke each other by sending gentle reminders of their team's superiority in Christmas cards, on Facebook and any other method they can think of. The rivalry continues, as I'm sure it will.

As the 2016 season deepened, I thought maybe this would be the year of the Cubs. Maybe Ernie and Ron will be smiling. Or perhaps at the end of the season we will just say "Maybe next year!" Either way, I'm sure Jack and Harry will have something to say about it.

Afterword

It is 1:33 a.m. I am sitting in a quiet living room. Husband is asleep. Cats are asleep. My only company is the television.

The Chicago Cubs are being presented with the Commissioner's Trophy. Yes, the trophy awarded to the team that has won the World Series. Let me say that again—"the team that has won the World Series." And that trophy is in the hands of the Chicago Cubs. The Cubs whose last Series win was 1908. The Cubs who have been known for years as the Lovable Losers. The Cubs whose fans' favorite phrase is "maybe next year."

Harry Caray predicted it when discussing the Cubs' season and their dashed hopes for a pennant in 1991. He said, "But that will come; sure as God made green apples. Someday the Chicago Cubs are going to be in the World Series. " Harry then went on to say it might be sooner than fans think.

Twenty sixteen was that year. The road to the series championship was not without its bumps. They had a great season and post-season. But being behind in the Series three games to one seemed like an impossible hurdle. Sure, other teams had done it. Baseball established the 2–3–2 format for the Series in 1925. Since that time, 34 teams have had a 3–1 advantage and those teams have won the Series 29 times. Not good odds. And the Cubs had to win the last two games on the road, at Cleveland.

So, being the Cubs, they did the impossible and forced a Game 7.

And what a game—the Cubbies sure do not make it easy on their fans.

I am sitting on the sofa trying to be quiet for the sleeping beings. At the end of the sixth inning, the Cubs are up 6–3. Do we dare hope? Maybe not. In inning eight, the Indians score three to tie the game. "Maybe next year" is running rampant through my mind. My shoulders tense. Both teams hold each other in the ninth. Good Lord, extra innings. What next? How about a rain delay. Will this never end? My head is starting to throb from the tension and the late hour. Pulling me through are the Tiger Buddies, a Facebook group of dedicated baseball fans, who are putting their Tiger loyalties aside for the night and pulling for the Cubs. Because that's what Tiger Buddies do. As I am almost giving up and heading for bed, an alert Tiger Buddy posts that the tarp will come up in about 15 minutes. I can do this.

The Cubs score two runs in the 10th, giving some breathing space to this weary fan. A two-run lead is nice. The Indians come back and score one run, making the score 8–7. After what seems an eternity, the third out comes to pass and the jubilant Cubs swarm the field. It has been about a five-hour game, much longer if you are a Cubs fan.

At 1:33 a.m., I am sitting quietly, drinking this all in. I should be screaming and jumping up and down for joy. I will do that tomorrow. For now, I am relishing the moment, barely able to believe it.

A lone tear slides down my cheek. And in the distance I hear the crunching of someone enjoying a green apple.

Dedicated to Dave. Keep cheering for those Sox, big brother.

Confessions of a Yet-to-Be Fan

Sam Watson

Baseball is the only game ever invented where the object is to keep anything from happening. That's not original with me; I read it somewhere. But it's always struck me as a fairly accurate description. Until maybe recently.

Six decades ago, when I was a middle-schooler, I was always the last one chosen for a pick-up baseball team at recess. Always. One day, for reasons I can neither remember nor imagine, they put me on the pitcher's mound. (Some teacher must have insisted on it.) As I pitched, everybody hit the ball— *everybody. Something was happening!* I honestly thought I was doing a splendid job, until my teammates explained to me that everybody getting a hit was not quite what they had in mind.

The recesses of my mind have just one other baseball memory. One day, somebody hit a high fly ball to deep left field. But that's where a young elementary teacher was leading her single-filed biddies to their own recess. The ball arced to earth and struck that poor woman right in her boobs, and she crumpled to the ground. She never knew what hit her, I think, but I'm pretty sure that she was never afterward a baseball fan.

Earlier still, much earlier, I wanted Mama to hurry up and have eight more sons, so we could have our own baseball team. That was not to be; I remained an only child.

When I was growing up, I did get myself a baseball. And, when I could afford it, I bought a good glove and had it for many years, just in case. It was a Wilson, kept supple with Neatsfoot oil. Sometimes I would take it out to play catch with myself, throwing high fly balls to nab, or rolling it down from the roof of our farmhouse. Very occasionally, instead of my farm chores after school, I would steal to my room, fetch ball and glove from the closet, lie on the bed and throw to the ceiling while I listened to the raucous Dizzy Dean calling a game on the radio. *Swing and a miss—strike three!* I have no idea why my parents put up with any of that, or with certain other activities of my growing up. Maybe it came from my being their only child.

Most summers I would spend a week or two working Down Home, the dairy farm where Mama had grown up as one of eight children. One day my first cousin Reed, a couple years older than me, let me go with him to a pick-up game with other farm boys. They must have been short-handed. I found myself in deep right field, where probably no ball would ever come. But one did. Should I try to catch the ball, or should I try to avoid stepping in the cow pies? (Is that what they mean by a *fielder's choice*?) I can't recall how I resolved the dilemma, but I did get the ball lobbed vaguely toward the infield.

There was another time when Reed and Uncle Powell decided to go to a game Holly Hill was playing someplace away. After milking the cows and putting them away for the evening, they climbed in the pick-up truck and headed out, listening to the play-by-play on the radio. But Holly Hill fell behind, so they turned back toward home. Then their team surged, so they turned around and headed toward the game again. I do not know if they ever got there.

Down Home consisted then of Uncle Powell, Reed, Reed's older sister Patsy, and their mother, Aunt Dodie. She was a strong woman, in her way; she had set up housekeeping in the old Felder home, and she endured a lifetime of the six Felder sisters, who could never be satisfied with whatever she was doing for their baby brother. Through the school year Aunt Dodie would try to get Reed to do his homework, and through the summer she would try to get him to wear shoes. Both efforts went pretty much without success. So did Aunt Dodie's attempt, once, to get her driver's license renewed. They stood her in front of a vision-testing machine and asked her what she saw. Nothing, absolutely nothing. Turned out, she was so short she was just seeing the top of the machine. If there had been a half-inch less of Aunt Dodie, she'd have legally been a dwarf. After Uncle Powell died she moved into their tiny lakefront concrete-block cabin near Eutawville. There she put up a plywood sign with a small person painted on it and the initials ELF. That was for her name, Eudora Lambert Felder. After she'd become an old lady, one Christmas Aunt Dodie asked her family to give her a pogo stick. They did, and she hopped all around the yard on it. I think she just wanted to see what the world would've looked like if she'd been taller. And she drove the ambulance for the local rescue squad. If you saw an ambulance or an automobile barreling toward you with nobody behind the wheel, that would be Aunt Dodie. She peered through the wheel because she couldn't see over it. But I suppose Aunt Dodie is a different story.

Back now to ball.

My friend Ken was a Renaissance man; he spent his life happily studying just about everything in the world. (Weeds were one of Ken's hobbies. He would forage for them, and then take specimens to talk at some gathering, illustrating how a particular plant shows up in Shakespeare.) But Ken knew nothing about baseball. One afternoon he was in a bar, peacefully sipping his beer. Two others sidled up and plopped on stools on either side. They started arguing about baseball, complete with all the requisite statistics. Then one of them turned to Ken and asked what he thought. Ken just shrugged his shoulders. Which brought this response: "My advice to you, buddy, is Get a Life." I've noticed that if you prick a true-blue baseball fan, he (or she) will spout statistics, out to three digits, together with some uninterruptable abbreviation. (What is ERA; PAB; RASP; LIPS; RMU; OBA; BF; SVO; OFA; CEBA? And why does anybody care? For that matter, could there be some historical factoid so obscure that *no* baseball fan knows it? I don't think so.)

By now it's clear, even to me, that I grew up pretty much baseball-deprived. And as an adult, I've seen just three major league games in person. The first was in Detroit. One night several of us decided to go see a game. It was Polish-American night, and Tiger Stadium was packed. Nolan Ryan was pitching against Mark Fidrych (why do I remember such things?). I came away convinced that big-city dwellers go to baseball games because that's a chance to swill overpriced beer, pee in a corner, see blue sky, and watch green grass grow. My second game was in Pittsburgh. It was the ninth inning when everyone suddenly got up and left. It seemed the pitcher had performed something called a balk, and that performance had somehow ended the game. My only other Major League game was in Los Angeles, watching the Dodgers play in their beautiful field with a background of mountains. I enjoyed being there, even though the Dodgers had committed the sin of leaving Brooklyn.

All that was then. This is now.

A couple months ago we were gathered for a family lunch at a Cracker Barrel in Columbia, South Carolina. Uncle Billy, my brother-in-law, may be the most die-hard fan the Gamecocks have. He's been known to follow the team to the College World Series in Omaha. They didn't go this year, and neither did Uncle Billy. But another South Carolina team *did* make it, the Chanticleers of Coastal Carolina. Uncle Billy told us how much he was enjoying watching them on TV. "They are good boys, and they're letting themselves just have FUN," he explained. Now, somebody just having FUN is something I rarely get to see, so when my wife Anne Knight and I returned home, we tuned in. From that point on, we didn't miss a pitch. They WERE having fun, and so were we. It lasted right through the last pitch of the last inning of the last game. The Chants won the game by a one-run margin, bringing back their school's first national championship in anything. They were helped by a mid-game surge, two runs scored when an Arizona infielder made two errors on the same play (Bless his heart!). And, it turned out later that a "safe" call for them at home plate probably should have been ruled an "out." But then, even perfection is seldom perfect.

So, watching this year's College World Series has been my most recent foray towards baseball. Until, that is, Chris Arvidson came to visit, towing two of my other former students with her. We didn't talk much about baseball, but I did pose a couple questions that had puzzled me. (Why is a baseball player always chewing—something? And spitting? And caressing his crotch? And what of that older guy who always stays in the dugout, leaning against the bar in front, spitting placidly, with eyes staring out at the field. Does he ever actually *do* anything?)

Then, a few days later, came The Book. From Chris (of course), used (of course!), but apparently it's mine to keep—and to mine, and to mind. It's a gem of a book, *Watching Baseball Smarter*, by somebody named Zack Hample. Thumbing through, I see it may address some of the questions I've been too embarrassed to ask. (See above.) Among my other questions: How come baseball has its own language? They've actually built a "stretch" into the seventh inning of every baseball game; is that a nod to the game's predictable boredom? And how can any sport be so thoroughly predictable that a player can be found guilty of an "error"? Why do uniforms usually look like pajamas? Why do fans stay loyal to teams that almost always lose? And why do taxpayers pay for new multi-million-dollar fancy stadiums that destroy neighborhoods and further stuff team owners' pockets? How has the game attracted such a cast of undeniably colorful characters, many of them butchers of the English language?

Years ago, I looked forward to the weekly NPR conversation between Bob Edwards and Red Barber. There was little about baseball, as I recall. It was mainly about what was blooming around Red Barber's retirement home in Tallahassee. But now, a quote in my new-old book stops me short. It is from Red Barber: "Baseball is dull only to dull minds." In recent weeks a fan with a philosophic turn of mind has explained this much to me: The attraction of baseball is not that anything is happening, because it usually isn't; it's the anticipation that something *might* happen, which it occasionally does.

Maybe so. Recently I tried to watch a Braves game on TV. Fans were sprawled about in the Denver stadium, apparently just soaking up sun. The announcers murmured into their microphones, as if they were afraid of waking up their TV viewers, or for that matter the players. They could've been calling a golf tournament, only more so. When the first inning finally ended the Braves were down by four runs, and the announcers seemed positively bored. That's when I took my wife out to an early dinner, telling her it was sort of a seventh-inning stretch between the Republican and Democratic conventions. (My wife is a political junkie.)

Clearly I have a ways to go. Maybe someday I'll enter the confines of a batter's box, bat in hand, just to see what that's like. I would want to face some reasonably competent pitcher. Doubtless I would never make a hit, but I wouldn't want to *be* hit.

Meanwhile I shall trudge on, in my own dull way. The next step is to actually finish reading the book. Then I shall need to make myself actually watch a game, all the way through.

Recently I did go to a baseball game, but I didn't exactly *watch* it. It was in Charleston, where the Class A RiverDogs were playing somebody from off. At "The Joe " (Joseph P. Riley, Jr. Park) it was Democrat night, and that's why I went. I walked in wearing my old Obama cap (yes, it's a *baseball* cap); pinned to its front (with two corsage pins), this:

Donald Duck is fun.

Donald Trump is QUACKED.

In my tattered backpack, many sheets of similar, home-written slogans of Hillary support, campaign literature which, to my relief, my fellow Dems received ungrumpily. Everyone seemed happy just to be there. (Full disclosure: a couple weeks later The Joe hosted a mock election. Trump won, two to one. Ah well.)

I don't know who won the game I went to. I think it was the guys from off, but nobody seemed much to care. Leaving the stadium there was lots of happy chatter. Just compare that to football, where young men mean to maim one another. Football fans leave a stadium with murder in their eyes, either the blood-lusty gloat of victors or, for the vanquished, the gloom of death-like defeat. Football is war. (I've heard that baseball does actually have an abbreviation, WAR, but don't ask me what it means.)

Baseball is different from football. I suppose baseball players are good at what they do, whatever that is. But they seem mostly to enjoy just chewing bubblegum, and spitting whatever, and jabbering. Someone famously said, "It ain't over 'til it's over." I'm beginning to think, baseball ain't EVER over, once it's been begun.

It's not the game itself; nothing much usually happens there. So why, from the distant past, do names and bits of memory stick in my mind, like cockleburs that can be fun to pick at, or an old itch that invites the occasional scratch?

I am a late learner, but there's something I'm beginning to see: Not "in" baseball exactly but "around" the game, something IS happening. It's the history; it's the stories. It's the *poetry* of it all, stupid!

Nothing Else Like It

CHRIS ARVIDSON

Nineteen eighty-four remains clear and distinct in my baseball-loving memories. I was working in Washington, D.C., in a political job, in a presidential campaign year—that experience alone might burn a permanent hole in your brain. But, 1984 was also the year my Detroit Tigers set the baseball world on fire. Baseball balanced out the overheated political atmosphere in which I found myself absorbed. Many of the friends I worked with were rabid fans, too. In my office we had Padres and Giants fans from California, New York Yankee die-hards, lifelong Mets gamers, Philly fanatics and everything in between.

Washington, D.C., didn't have a Major League team in 1984. The Senators were long gone. The Nationals but a distant hope. To fill this baseball void, a bunch of us had gotten together and bought season tickets to the closest team to us, the Baltimore Orioles. The scheme worked fabulously. Each of our consortium members had a different favorite team, so we rarely clashed over tickets for a particular series. In February, when pitchers and catchers reported to Spring Training, we'd have a big party, eat hot dogs, wear our favorite teams' gear and draw lots to pick our games. There were ten of us and we had four seats to every home game.

The Oriole's old park at the time, Memorial Stadium, was located smack dab in the middle of an old middle class Baltimore neighborhood. It wasn't set out in its own complex or placed in a high-density commercial location the way baseball stadiums are now. We'd drive in from D.C. on the Baltimore Washington Parkway, through neighborhoods of white steps, past people selling bushel baskets of crabs on the corners. You parked on the neighborhood streets for the game, not in vast color-coded and numbered lots, or echoing concrete parking garages. The beer was National Premium at the park. The "Oh" in the National Anthem's line: "Oh say does that Star Spangled..." was always shouted "O" and it was the era of Earl the Pearl Weaver kicking dirt and Eddie Murray and Jim Palmer. Good times.

As fun as Orioles baseball was, 1984 was all–Tigers all the time for me. My team. From the get-go the Tigers tore it up. In April they came out of the box setting an 18–2 record, winning the first nine. After 30 games, they were 26–4, after 40 games, 36–5. Tiger baseball was completely and utterly glorious to watch.

I was an obnoxious brat at the office. I'd ask the boss, a huge Orioles fan, "Hey did you hear about that game last night?" Every. Damn. Day. People started putting cartoons on my door, writing my name over Sparky Anderson's quotes. The relatively few times the Tigers lost that year, I'm sure many of my colleagues were hoping it would be the beginning of my comeuppance. Surely the Tigers would settle down, have a slide, hit the skids. Tank.

A few blocks away, over on Capitol Hill, where people from Michigan worked in House and Senate offices, there were fellow Tiger fans on hand. So numerous and loyal were they that a Tiger fan club was formed called The Mayo Smith Society. Smith had been the Tiger manager in 1968, the last time they won the World Series. Mayo Smith Society members would get together in the House of Representatives' employee cafeteria and talk Tigers. And when the Tigers played in Baltimore, we members would get a bus to take to the games. We were serious fans.

One year, a Wall Street Journal reporter, Paul Cox, a Tiger fan himself, wrote a story for his paper about the club. He rode on the bus with us to a Tigers vs. Baltimore game and wrote about the trivia contest we had on the way. Members would try to come up with the best stumpers for club members to solve—we had some major trivia and numbers geeks among us. I was so proud my question made that Wall Street Journal story. It was: "What Tiger catcher had to leave a Cleveland game after being hit with a basket of green tomatoes thrown from the upper deck?" The answer? It was catcher Birdie Tebbetts on September 27, 1940. According to my source material, *This Date in Detroit Tigers History,* by John C. Hawkins, the Cleveland fans were mighty unruly that day, throwing fruit, vegetables and eggs as the Tigers clinched the pennant, beating Bob Feller 2–0.

The Mayo Smith Society is still going strong. My husband and I went to the annual spring luncheon in Detroit in 2016. It was sold out. More than 100+ Tiger-geared fanatics listened to Mickey Lolich, one of Mayo Smith's 1968 World Series greats, a pitching legend. I didn't ask Mickey for an autograph, but I did go up and talk to him briefly and my husband snapped a picture of us. Mickey is a peach of a guy, very much old school (he thinks pitch counts are for wimps), completely not a baseball diva. And my husband, who was indulging me mightily by coming to the luncheon, and who had clearly not looked forward to the occasion, actually ended up having a wonderful time. It's impossible to not like Mickey Lolich.

To the delight of Mayo Smith fans everywhere, the 1984 Tigers quickly became odds-on favorites for the World Series. About halfway through the season, I even started paying attention to the National League, something I hardly ever did back then, to keep track of how October might shape up. And my enthusiasm and the Tigers' stellar play became contagious. At work, I dragged fans of other (inferior) teams along with me for the Tigers' ride, making many converts to Detroit fandom. It wasn't difficult. We had great personalities on that team, like Kirk Gibson "Gibby" and the dynamite infield combo of Alan Trammell and Lou Whittaker. And seriously, who didn't love Tiger Manager Sparky Anderson? He was scrappy and feisty and crafty and the team clearly responded to him. He was also a nice man by all counts; certainly he was to me.

I got to meet Sparky one afternoon in Lakeland, Florida, at Tiger Spring Training, I clutched a program and pen and stood at the fence at the end of a game. That is, I stood with a bunch of little kids. They were all hollering "Sparky, Sparky!" I tried to maintain at least a smidgen of adult decorum, but when one of the grounds people opened that gate and waved us onto the field where Sparky had just finished talking to a pitcher, I ran with those 8-year-olds out there. Yes I did. Sparky cheerfully talked to all the kids and signed autographs, patiently looking into each one of their faces, listening. When he got to me, he had to look up because I'm a good foot taller than the kids and had a couple inches on Sparky, too. He was surprised and started laughing, saying, "how'd you get in this crowd?" as he autographed my program. I've looked everywhere for that autograph, and I can't find it, which is really sad because the next autograph I asked for at Spring Training went horribly the opposite way.

Any Detroit fan of my era is automatically an Al Kaline worshipper. Hell, he's known as "Mr. Tiger," he's a Hall of Famer, a former Tiger broadcaster, still a team official—you name it, and Kaline has done it in the Tiger organization. One March afternoon in Lakeland I waited outside the broadcast booth in the stands for my hero to come out after the game he'd just called with his partner George Kell. They exited the booth and I approached Kaline with a program and pen outstretched in my shaking hand. I was polite in the extreme. Very respectful. I called him "Mr. Kaline."

He blew me off like something stuck on his shoe.

So utterly deflating was his callous reaction to my perfectly normal request for an autograph, I thought I would burst into tears. Kell, who was walking right behind Kaline was clearly embarrassed at his colleague's behavior and took one look at my face and stopped and sat down on the bleachers right there with me and talked for a good ten minutes. George Kell was a class guy all the way. I've never asked for another autograph in my life. I don't want to get crushed like that ever again. And, by the end of 1984, I had some much better souvenirs than some old Al Kaline autograph anyway.

The regular season powered to a close and the Tigers continued their record-breaking ways. Things were also heating up at work—big elections, late nights, crazy times. But the Tigers were never off my mind. In mid–September, with the pennant clinched, I was anticipating the World Series. I thought "Oh my god. It is really going to happen." And remember, in 1984, you couldn't just flip a cable channel on or subscribe to MLB TV. You had to do this thing called reading the box scores in newspapers the next day. Maybe sometimes, if you got lucky and the wind and atmosphere were right, you could pick up a late night few minutes of Ernie Harwell on AM radio from WJR in Detroit. I was looking forward to seeing my Tigers on television for the World Series.

Then the unthinkable happened. A few days before the series was to begin my boss gave me some potentially thrilling news. Our chairman would, naturally, have access to World Series tickets. And while the California tickets would be quickly dispersed since that was his home state, there might, possibly, small chance, be a possibility that there wouldn't be enough "important people" who wanted to go to Detroit, and if that might, possibly, small chance did in fact happen, I, Chris Arvidson, would get the tickets.

But I still had problems to fix—I needed to see if I could get myself, last minute, to Detroit on my own. The game tickets were free, but not the plane, and I wouldn't know if I had the tickets until the day before. Did I want to take dibs on this maybe, possibly, small chance deal? Oh hell yes.

Then I got the word. I had the tickets. I had a bag already packed. I raced to the airport and got a cheapo Peoples Express flight to Detroit, through Newark, from National Airport. But, there was one more hitch to this whole thing…. I had to get to the Renaissance Center in downtown Detroit by 4:00 p.m. to get the tickets from Major League Baseball's chief lobbyist. If I didn't get there in time he was going to give them away to someone else.

Of course the lines were long at the airports. The planes were late. Newark was a nightmare and the Peoples Express cheapo flights staff, the few who actually seemed to be working there, were maddeningly casual about actually boarding and leaving and arriving on time. When I got to Detroit's airport I ran all the way through it and out to the curb and got in a cab and leaned over the seat to the nice man driving and said, "Look. I don't have a lot of money, but I'll give you a really big tip if you can somehow get me to the Ren Cen by 4 because I've got World Series tickets waiting for me there if I get there in time, and, and…"

Of course he took it as a personal challenge. He said, "OK, just lean back in your seat. We're gonna do this." I did more than lean back. Before we were out of the airport, I was ducking down in the seat. I didn't want to see. The one time I did peek out the window, my cab driver was passing someone on the left hand shoulder of the freeway. He got me to the Ren Cen at 3:50. I gave him $20, a veritable fortune to me at the time.

I raced in the door, hit the up elevator button, slapped the "close door" switch and crept up and up the Renaissance Center to the floor of the magic baseball suite. I had made it in time. The tickets were cheerfully handed over. On the way back down, just a few minutes later, I clutched in my hand four tickets to each of Games 3, 4 and 5 of the 1984 World Series.

I felt like I was holding a million dollars. I wanted to stuff the tickets in my bra. I was afraid to take them out of my hands and put them in anything so flimsy as a wallet or my purse. I ran out of the elevator, into the lobby and straight into a phone booth. Now that I had the tickets in my hand, I could call my family and friends and say, "Hey, if you're not doing anything this weekend, wanna see the Tigers in the World Series?" Section 105. Row 10. Lower box seats in lovely Tiger Stadium. Michigan and Trumball.

Good old Tiger Stadium. All painted like a great white elephant on the outside. All dark and dingy and cool and smelling like grilled Italian sausages with onions and green peppers and popcorn and old sticky spilled Stroh's on the inside. Just to breathe it in…. Who wouldn't want to go there anytime, much less for the World Series? My local high school friends, those still living in the Detroit area, loved me mightily that weekend. My dad and my sister and my brother-in-law did, too; they drove down from up north to come to one of the games.

It is very difficult to describe the feeling of watching games in person at a World Series, when you are so invested in one of the teams. Once in a lifetime? Sure. Roller coaster ride? Yep. Each game was like a whole novel in a single outing, a life story told in nine innings. The agony and the ecstasy? You'd better believe it. At one point I went to a phone booth in the stadium and called a Michigan friend who was hard at work back in D.C., and held the phone out for him to hear the roar of the crowd. I drank Stroh's, bought a pair of furry Tiger ears on a headband and I don't think I sat down in my seat for any of the innings in any of those three games. We cursed the Padres. We screamed our lungs out until we were hoarse for our team.

The Tigers won the World Series in five games in 1984. I was there. I was there when Gibby blasted Rich "the Goose" Gossage's pitch into the stands for three runs, rightly figuring that the Goose wouldn't be able to resist pitching to him. I was there when Aurelio Lopez "Senor Smoke" got the win and Willie Hernandez took the save. And I was there when people from the stands poured onto the field and began chopping out pieces of turf to take home. I didn't run out onto the field, but those folks who did started throwing pieces up to people dancing for joy in the stands and I got one of those. Now that's a souvenir.

After the screaming and crying and hugging strangers and horn honking and general mayhem of joyous celebration, I got back to the airport hotel where I was staying before my early a.m. flight back to D.C. Once there, I retrieved that piece of turf from my purse and carefully wrapped it in a damp washcloth and put that little package inside the hotel's plastic laundry bag and then into my suitcase.

When I got on the plane home, I was seated way in the very back. I marched proudly down the aisle with my Tiger ears still on and got applause the whole way to my seat. I wore those ears all the way home and I wore them to work on Monday, too. I planted that piece of turf in a pot and had it for many years, until one summer when I went on vacation it finally died. The grass was from the outfield and my sister always said it was one of the spots where Gibby spat. I've always believed that was true.

About the Contributors

Chris **Arvidson** is a writer and baseball super-fan. She's the coeditor of *Mountain Memoirs* and *Reflections on the New River*, and a cofounder of the writing salon Wordkeepers. She earned a BA from Olivet College, an MA from the University of North Carolina at Charlotte and an MFA from Goucher College.

Robyn **Barberry** earned an MFA in creative nonfiction from Goucher College in 2011. She writes a blog called "Unconditional" for *The Catholic Review* and teaches art at St. Joan of Arc School in Aberdeen, Maryland.

Joseph **Bathanti** is a former poet laureate of North Carolina (2012–14) and recipient of the 2016 North Carolina Award in Literature. He is the author of ten books of poetry, including *Concertina,* winner of the 2014 Roanoke Chowan Prize. He teaches at Appalachian State University.

Douglas J. **Butler** is an award-winning writer and photographer living in northwestern North Carolina. An adventure traveler and independent scholar, he has written numerous articles and two books that include his photography: *A Walk Atop America* and *North Carolina Civil War Monuments.*

Jody **DiPerna** lives in Pittsburgh and writes about outsider sports and their impact on community. She is working on a larger project about the death of a small Western Pennsylvania mill town. She has written for numerous Pittsburgh newspapers and magazines, as well as several national media outlets.

Henry **Doss** is a former banker who works as a singer-songwriter, recording artist, writer and business consultant. He earned an MA at the University of North Carolina at Charlotte, where he also served as the Executive in Residence for the College of Liberal Arts and Sciences.

L.C. **Fiore** is an award-winning short-story writer and editor. His work has appeared on NPR, *TriQuarterly Review,* The Good Men Project, and in various baseball publications. He is the communications director for the North Carolina Writers' Network.

Nancy A. **Gutierrez** is a professor of English and the dean of the College of Liberal Arts and Sciences at the University of North Carolina at Charlotte. She has a Ph.D.

and MA in English from the University of Chicago and a BA in English from Denison University.

Rachel Pfennig **Hales** has been interested in the arts from an early age. She earned an MFA from Goucher College, an MA from National University, and an BA from DePauw University. In addition to writing, she works in live event production for concert touring.

Karen **Hamilton** teaches English as a Second Language to adults in San Diego, California. She played NCAA softball for the Pomona-Pitzer Sagehens. She also served in the Peace Corps in Ukraine and taught English to professional baseball players in the Dodger minor league system.

Diana Nelson **Jones** lives in Pittsburgh, where she is a reporter and columnist for the *Pittsburgh Post-Gazette*. A graduate of Ohio University in Athens, with a BS in journalism, she has worked for the *Huntington Herald-Dispatch* (WV) and the now-defunct *Tulsa Tribune*. She is a lifelong fan of the Pittsburgh Pirates.

Caroline Kane **Kenna** is a member of the Charlotte Writers' Club and a former newspaper reporter. She earned a BA in history from King College and a BA in journalism from Memphis State University. Her work has been published in *Reflections on the New River* and *Above the Fold*.

Stephen **Kirk** is the former editor-in-chief at John F. Blair, and the author of *Voices from the Outer Banks*, *Scribblers* and *First in Flight*. His writing has also appeared in the "Best American Short Stories" series and other volumes. He lives near Winston-Salem, North Carolina.

Kevin **Kirkland** has worked as an editor for 32 years, mostly at the *Pittsburgh Post-Gazette*. He is the newspaper's Magazine and Homes editor, and is also the author of *Lucky Bats,* a children's book about Elijah Miller, a batboy for the Homestead Grays. He has a BA from St. Bonaventure University.

Lawrence **Lawson** lives in San Diego, California, and is an associate professor at Palomar College. He is a returned Peace Corps volunteer (Ukraine, 2005–07), and has published textbooks with Oxford University Press. He is a die-hard San Francisco Giants fan.

Rebecca Bratcher **Laxton** earned a Psy.S from Eastern Kentucky University and a BA from Georgetown College. She worked as a school psychologist in Boone County, Kentucky, and was the Kentucky School Psychologist of the Year in 1999. She is working toward an MA in liberal studies at the University of North Carolina at Charlotte.

Elizabeth Scott **Leik** has taught writing at Loyola University, Maryland, and Goucher College, and is a writer and editor focusing on travel, memoir, profiles, and education. She has an MFA from Goucher College, an MS from Johns Hopkins University, and a BA from Kenyon College.

David E. **Malehorn** is a regular contributor to the *Pittsburgh Post-Gazette*. His 35-year career as a scientist has been almost as diverse as his extracurricular activities.

He has pursued microbiology, molecular biology and biotechnology in academic and entrepreneurial positions.

Glenn B. **Marcus** is a documentary filmmaker in Washington, D.C., who served 13 years at the National Endowment for the Humanities and eventually produced and wrote several PBS national prime time programs, including a national Emmy nominated program. He is on the faculty at Johns Hopkins University.

Jean C. **O'Brien** is ordained in the Christian Church (Disciples of Christ) in the United States and Canada. She has worked nearly 30 years as a choral director and has served as a pastor since 2001. She has a BA from Olivet College, and a M.Div. from Christian Theological Seminary in Indianapolis, Indiana.

Brendan **O'Meara** is the author of *Six Weeks in Saratoga*, and is a Push Cart–nominated essayist and an award-winning magazine writer. He hosts *#CNF*, a podcast where he speaks with writers, journalists, and filmmakers about creating works of nonfiction.

Juanita **Ramsey-Jevne** is a former teacher and began her writing career by creating an original musical each year for Five Acre School, a private school she cofounded with her husband. After retiring, she earned an MFA in creative nonfiction from Goucher College.

Ellyn **Ritterskamp** edits and designs in newspaper publishing and teaches practical ethics at the University of North Carolina at Charlotte, where she earned a BA and two master's degrees. She has visited all of the home parks in Major League Baseball, the South Atlantic League and the Carolina League.

Tom **Stanton** is an associate professor of journalism at University of Detroit Mercy. He is the author of seven books of nonfiction, including the 2016 *New York Times* sports bestseller *Terror in the City of Champions*. He won the Casey Award for *The Final Season* and was a Quill Award finalist for *Ty and The Babe*.

Victoria **Stopp**'s work has appeared in *Backpacker Magazine, Agnes Scott: The Magazine, Atlanta CityMag, The Atlanta Journal-Constitution,* and several other publications. She lives in Florida and is the author of a forthcoming nonfiction book about surviving chronic pain.

Becky Mason **Stragand** is a retired educator who pursues writing full-time. She is a former columnist for the *Morganton News Herald* and the *Ashe Mountain Times.* Her work has appeared in *Mountain Memoirs* and *Reflections on the New River.*

Julie E. **Townsend** has been a writer, a university instructor, and a real estate broker. She coedited *Mountain Memoirs* and *Reflections on the New River* and has also written a novel, *Seafood Jesus.* She is also a published short story writer and cofounder of the writers' salon Wordkeepers.

Stephen P. **Ward** is a university administrator who has worked as a communicator in a variety of settings, in a career rooted in journalism. He is a graduate of Michigan State University and earned an MA from The American University in Washington, D.C.

Sam **Watson** is a professor emeritus of English at University of North Carolina at Charlotte. He graduated from Wofford College (with one year at Queen's University, Belfast, Northern Ireland), earned an MA in English at the University of Virginia and his Ph.D. at the University of Iowa.

David **Wolin** is a graduate of Tufts University and Harvard Law School and is the owner of Old York Cellars, a boutique winery in Ringoes, New Jersey. He worked as a real estate finance attorney for many years in New York City, before "retiring" to the countryside.

Index